JEAN CRAIGHEAD GEORGE
One Day in the Tropical Rain Forest
ILLUSTRATED BY GARY ALLEN

DISCARDED

Here's all the great literature in this grade level of *Celebrate Reading!*

MARY POPPINS
REVISED EDITION
P.L. TRAVERS

NUMBER THE STARS

CLASS PRESIDENT

MR. MYSTERIOUS & COMPANY

Flights of Fancy
Journeys of the Imagination

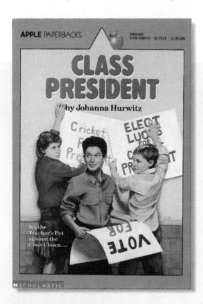

Class President
from the novel by Johanna Hurwitz
✺ Kentucky Bluegrass Award
✺ South Carolina Children's
Book Award

What a Wild Idea
by Louis Sabin

**I'm Tipingee, She's Tipingee,
We're Tipingee, Too**
by Caroline Feller Bauer
✺ Christopher Award Author

**The Voice of Africa in
American Music**
by Jim Haskins
✺ Coretta Scott King Award Author

The Third Gift
by Jan Carew
Illustrations by Leo and Diane Dillon

**Ashanti to Zulu:
African Traditions**
from the book by Margaret Musgrove
Illustrations by Leo and Diane Dillon
✺ Boston Globe-Horn Book Award
✺ Caldecott Medal

Mary Poppins
from the novel by P. L. Travers
✺ Nene Award

Catwings
by Ursula K. Le Guin
✺ Children's Choice
✺ Irma Simonton Black Award

Featured Poet
Natalia Belting

Before Your Very Eyes

A World of Nature

Only Fiona
from the novel by Beverly Keller

Urban Roosts: Where Birds Nest in the City
by Barbara Bash
✹ Teachers' Choice

One Day in the Tropical Rain Forest
from the novel by
Jean Craighead George
✹ Notable Social Studies Trade Book

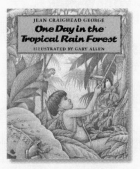

All Upon a Sidewalk
by Jean Craighead George
✹ Newbery Award Author

Turtle in July
from the collection by
Marilyn Singer
Illustrations by Jerry Pinkney
✹ New York Times Best Illustrated
✹ Outstanding Science Trade Book

The Desert Is Theirs
from the poem by Byrd Baylor
Illustrated by Peter Parnall
✹ Caldecott Honor Book
✹ Boston Globe-Horn Book Award

The Growin' of Paul Bunyan
by William J. Brooke
✹ Children's Choice
✹ ALA Notable Children's Book

The Book of Eagles
from the book by Helen
Roney Sattler
✹ Outstanding Science Trade Book
✹ ALA Notable Children's Book

Isaac Asimov's Futureworld: Travel on Earth
by Isaac Asimov
✹ The Washington Post/Children's
Book Guild Nonfiction
Award Author

Featured Poets
Marilyn Singer
Byrd Baylor
George David Weiss
Bob Thiele

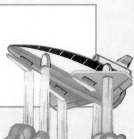

Many People, Many Voices
Stories of America

The Long Winter
from the novel by
Laura Ingalls Wilder
Illustrations by Garth Williams
✳ Newbery Honor Book

Samuel's Choice
by Richard Berleth
✳ Notable Social Studies Trade Book

Lincoln: A Photobiography
from the book by Russell Freedman
✳ Newbery Medal
✳ ALA Notable Children's Book
✳ Notable Social Studies Trade Book

Cowboys of the Wild West
from the book by Russell Freedman
✳ ALA Notable Children's Book
✳ Notable Social Studies Trade Book

Hector Lives in the United States Now
from the book by Joan Hewett
✳ Notable Social Studies Trade Book

Anastasia
by Shannon Liffland

Pecos Bill's Widow-Maker
by Margaret Hodges

The Tales of Uncle Remus
from the collection by Julius Lester
Illustrations by Jerry Pinkney
✳ ALA Notable Children's Book
✳ Notable Social Studies Trade Book

Her Seven Brothers
by Paul Goble
✳ Children's Choice
✳ Teachers' Choice
✳ *School Library Journal* Best Book

Featured Poets
Duke Redbird
Linh To Sinh My Bui

Within My Reach

The Important Things in Life

Thin Air
from the novel by David Getz

Skybird to the High Heavens
by Nancy White Carlstrom
Illustrations by José Ortega

Mr. Mysterious & Company
from the novel by Sid Fleischman
✴ Spring Book Festival Award

**The Great American
Gold Rush**
from the book by Rhoda Blumberg
✴ ALA Notable Children's Book
✴ Teachers' Choice

Oh, Susanna
Traditional Song

**Black Heroes of the
Wild West**
from the book by Ruth Pelz

**The Search for the
Magic Lake**
retold by Genevieve Barlow

The Magic Sieve
play by Irene N. Watts from a
Japanese folk tale
Illustrations by Satoru Igarashi

Featured Poet
Arnold Adoff

Handle with Care

Making a Difference

All About Sam
from the novel by Lois Lowry
❋ Mark Twain Award

Number the Stars
from the novel by Lois Lowry
❋ Newbery Medal
❋ ALA Notable Children's Book
❋ Teachers' Choice
❋ Notable Social Studies Trade Book

Jessi's Secret Language
from the novel by Ann M. Martin

Take a Walk in Their Shoes
from the biography by
Glennette Tilley Turner
❋ Notable Social Studies Trade Book

Dorothea Lange: Life Through the Camera
from the biography by
Milton Meltzer
❋ Boston Globe-Horn Book
Award Author

Featured Poets
Ouida Sebestyen
Danny Williams

Ask Me Again Tomorrow
Growing and Changing

La Bamba
by Gary Soto
✳ Judy Lopez Memorial Award

El Chino
by Allen Say
✳ Notable Social Studies Trade Book

Little by Little
from the autobiography by
Jean Little
✳ Boston Globe-Horn Book Award
✳ ALA Notable Children's Book

Justin and the Best Biscuits in the World
from the novel by
Mildred Pitts Walter
✳ Coretta Scott King Award

Stories from the Blue Road
from the novel by Emily Crofford
✳ Friends of American Writers
Juvenile Book Award Author

Little Green Men
by Barry B. Longyear

Day of the Earthlings
by Eve Bunting
✳ California Young Reader
Medal Author

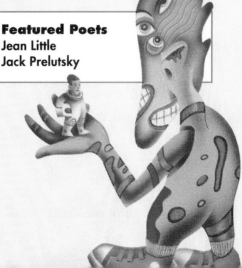

JUSTIN and the
BEST BISCUITS
IN THE WORLD

MILDRED PITTS WALTER

LITTLE BY
LITTLE
A Writer's Education

JEAN LITTLE

Featured Poets
Jean Little
Jack Prelutsky

Many People,
Many Voices

STORIES OF AMERICA

Titles in This Set

Flights of Fancy
Before Your Very Eyes
Many People, Many Voices
Within My Reach
Handle With Care
Ask Me Again Tomorrow

About the Cover
The cover artists, Bill and Kay Burlingham, spent
hundreds of hours creating the quilt you see
photographed on the front cover. Bill photographed
the children and transferred the photos to fabric,
while Kay hand sewed the blocks of fabric together.
They called this a project of love and hated to part
with the quilt once it was done.

ISBN 0-673-80053-9

Acknowledgments appear on page 128.

5678910RRS999897969594

Many People, Many Voices

STORIES OF AMERICA

ScottForesman
A Division of HarperCollins*Publishers*

contents

Stories from America's Past

GENRE STUDY

C·6 An Errand to Town
from The Long Winter
Historical fiction by Laura Ingalls Wilder
Illustrations by Garth Williams

C·18 Samuel's Choice
Historical fiction by Richard Berleth
Illustrations by James Watling

Russell Freedman, An American Author

AUTHOR STUDY

C·42 The Mysterious Mr. Lincoln
from Lincoln: A Photobiography
Biography by Russell Freedman

C·50 A Word from the Author
Essay by Russell Freedman

C·54 A Cow Herder on Horseback
from Cowboys of the Wild West
Expository nonfiction by Russell Freedman

A Land of Many People

C·64 Hector
from Hector Lives in the United States Now
Nonfiction by Joan Hewett

C·70   Anastasia
Essay by Shannon Liffland

C·72   Saigon of Vietnam
Poem by Linh To Sinh My Bui

C·74   My moccasins have not walked
Poem by Duke Redbird

American Tales of Spunk

C·76   Pecos Bill's Widow-Maker
Tall tale by Margaret Hodges

C·94   A Word from the Author
Essay by Julius Lester

C·96   Brer Rabbit Goes Back to Mr. Man's Garden
from The Tales of Uncle Remus
Folk tale by Julius Lester
Illustrations by Jerry Pinkney

C·104   Her Seven Brothers
Cheyenne myth
Written and illustrated by Paul Goble

STUDENT RESOURCES

C·118   Books to Enjoy

C·120   Literary Terms

C·122   Glossary

AN ERRAND
TO TOWN

BY LAURA INGALLS WILDER

ILLUSTRATED BY GARTH WILLIAMS

C·6

ONE MORNING in September the grass was white with frost. It was only a light frost that melted as soon as sunshine touched it. It was gone when Laura looked out at the bright morning. But at breakfast Pa said that such an early frost was surprising.

"Will it hurt the hay?" Laura asked him, and he said, "Oh, no. Such a light frost will only make it dry faster when it's cut. But I'd better get a hustle on, for it won't be long now till it's too late to make hay."

He was hustling so fast that afternoon that he hardly stopped to drink when Laura brought him the water jug. He was mowing in Big Slough.

"You cover it up, Half-Pint," he said, handing back the jug. "I'm bound and determined to get this patch mowed before sundown." He chirruped to Sam and David and they started again, drawing the whirring machine. Then suddenly the machine gave a clattering kind of yelp and Pa said, "Whoa!"

Laura hurried to see what had happened. Pa was looking at the cutter-bar. There was a gap in the row of bright steel points. The cutter-bar had lost one of its teeth. Pa picked up the pieces, but they could not be mended.

"There's no help for it," Pa said. "It means buying another section."

There was nothing to say to that. Pa thought a minute and said, "Laura, I wish you'd go to town and get it. I don't want to lose the time. I can keep on mowing, after a fashion, while you're gone. Be as quick as you can. Ma will give you the five cents to pay for it. Buy it at Fuller's Hardware."

"Yes, Pa," Laura said. She dreaded going to town because so many people were there. She was not exactly afraid, but strange eyes looking at her made her uncomfortable.

She had a clean calico dress to wear and she had shoes. While she hurried to the house, she thought that Ma might let her wear her Sunday hair-ribbon and perhaps Mary's freshly ironed sunbonnet.

"I have to go to town, Ma," she said, rushing in breathless.

Carrie and Mary listened while she explained and even Grace looked up at her with big, sober blue eyes.

"I will go with you to keep you company," Carrie volunteered.

"Oh, can she, Ma?" Laura asked.

"If she can be ready as soon as you are," Ma gave permission.

Quickly they changed to fresh dresses and put on their stockings and shoes. But Ma saw no reason for hair-ribbons on a week day and she said Laura must wear her own sunbonnet.

"It would be fresher," Ma said, "if you took care to keep it so." Laura's bonnet was limp from hanging down her back and the strings were limp too. But that was Laura's own fault.

Ma gave her five cents from Pa's pocketbook and with Carrie she hurried away toward town.

They followed the road made by Pa's wagon-wheels, past the well, down the dry, grassy slope into Big Slough, and on between the tall slough-grasses to the slope up on the other side. The whole shimmering prairie seemed strange then. Even the wind blowing the grasses had a wilder sound. Laura liked that and she wished they did not have to go into town where the false fronts of the buildings stood up square-topped to pretend that the stores behind them were bigger than they were.

Neither Laura nor Carrie said a word after they came to Main Street. Some men were on the store porches and two teams with wagons were tied to the hitching posts. Lonely, on the other side of Main Street, stood Pa's store building. It was rented and two men sat inside it talking.

Laura and Carrie went into the hardware store. Two men were sitting on nail kegs and one on a plow. They stopped talking and looked at Laura and Carrie. The wall behind the counter glittered with tin pans and pails and lamps.

Laura said, "Pa wants a mowing-machine section, please."

The man on the plow said, "He's broke one, has he?" and Laura said, "Yes, sir."

She watched him wrap in paper the sharp and shining three-cornered tooth. He must be Mr. Fuller. She gave him the five cents and, taking the package in her hand, she said, "Thank you," and walked out with Carrie.

That was over. But they did not speak until they had walked out of town. Then Carrie said, "You did that beautifully, Laura."

"Oh, it was just buying something," Laura replied.

"I know, but I feel funny when people look at me. I feel . . . not scared, exactly . . ." Carrie said.

"There's nothing to be scared of," Laura said. "We mustn't ever be scared." Suddenly she told Carrie, "I feel the same way."

"Do you, really? I didn't know that. You don't act like it. I always feel so safe when you're there," Carrie said.

"You are safe when I'm there," Laura answered. "I'd take care of you. Anyway, I'd try my best."

"I know you would," Carrie said.

It was nice, walking together. To take care of their shoes, they did not walk in the dusty wheel-tracks. They walked on the harder strip in the middle where only horses' hoofs had discouraged the grass. They were not walking hand in hand, but they felt as if they were.

Ever since Laura could remember, Carrie had been her little sister. First she had been a tiny baby, then

she had been Baby Carrie, then she had been a
clutcher and tagger, always asking "Why?" Now she
was ten years old, old enough to be really a sister.
And they were out together, away from even Pa and
Ma. Their errand was done and off their minds, and
the sun was shining, the wind was blowing, the prairie
spread far all around them. They felt free and
independent and comfortable together.

"It's a long way around to where Pa is," Carrie
said. "Why don't we go this way?" and she pointed
toward the part of the slough where they could see Pa
and the horses.

Laura answered, "That way's through the slough."

"It isn't wet now, is it?" Carrie asked.

"All right, let's," Laura answered. "Pa didn't say to
go by the road, and he did say to hurry."

So they did not follow the road that turned to cross
the slough. They went straight on into the tall
slough grass.

At first it was fun. It was rather like going into the
jungle-picture in Pa's big green book. Laura pushed
ahead between the thick clumps of grass-stems that
gave way rustling and closed again behind Carrie.
The millions of coarse grass-stems and their slender
long leaves were greeny-gold and golden-green in
their own shade. The earth was crackled with dryness
underfoot, but a faint smell of damp lay under the hot
smell of the grass. Just above Laura's head the grass-
tops swished in the wind, but down at their roots was
a stillness, broken only where Laura and Carrie went
wading through it.

"Where's Pa?" Carrie asked suddenly.

Laura looked around at her. Carrie's peaked little face was pale in the shade of the grass. Her eyes were almost frightened.

"Well, we can't see him from here," Laura said. They could see only the leaves of the thick grass waving, and the hot sky overhead. "He's right ahead of us. We'll come to him in a minute."

She said it confidently but how could she know where Pa was? She could not even be sure where she was going, where she was taking Carrie. The smothering heat made sweat trickle down her throat and her backbone, but she felt cold inside. She remembered the children near Brookings, lost in the prairie grass. The slough was worse than the prairie. Ma had always been afraid that Grace would be lost in this slough.

She listened for the whirr of the mowing machine, but the sound of the grasses filled her ears. There was nothing in the flickering shadows of their thin leaves blowing and tossing higher than her eyes, to tell her where the sun was. The grasses' bending and swaying did not even tell the direction of the wind. Those clumps of grass would hold up no weight at all. There was nothing, nothing anywhere that she could climb to look out above them, to see beyond them and know where she was.

"Come along, Carrie," she said cheerfully. She must not frighten Carrie.

Carrie followed trustfully but Laura did not know where she was going. She could not even be sure that she was walking straight. Always a clump of grass was in her way; she must go to right or left. Even if she went to the right of one clump of grass and to the left of the next clump, that did not mean that she was not going in a circle. Lost people go in circles and many of them never find their way home.

The slough went on for a mile or more of bending, swaying grasses, too tall to see beyond, too yielding to climb. It was wide. Unless Laura walked straight ahead they might never get out of it.

"We've gone so far, Laura," Carrie panted. "Why don't we come to Pa?"

"He ought to be right around here somewhere," Laura answered. She could not follow their own trail back to the safe road. Their shoes left almost no tracks on the heat-baked mud, and the grasses, the endless swaying grasses with their low leaves hanging dried and broken, were all alike.

Carrie's mouth opened a little. Her big eyes looked up at Laura and they said, "I know. We're lost." Her mouth shut without a word. If they were lost, they were lost. There was nothing to say about it.

"We'd better go on," Laura said.

"I guess so. As long as we can," Carrie agreed.

They went on. They must surely have passed the place where Pa was mowing. But Laura could not be sure of anything. Perhaps if they thought they turned back, they would really be going farther away. They could only go on. Now and then they stopped and wiped their sweating faces. They were terribly thirsty but there was no water. They were very tired from pushing through the grasses. Not one single push seemed hard, but going on was harder than trampling hay. Carrie's thin little face was gray-white, she was so tired.

Then Laura thought that the grasses ahead were thinner. The shade seemed lighter there and the tops of the grasses against the sky seemed fewer. And suddenly she saw sunshine, yellow beyond the dark grass stems. Perhaps there was a pond there. Oh! perhaps, perhaps there was Pa's stubble field and the mowing machine and Pa.

She saw the hay stubble in the sunshine, and she saw haycocks dotting it. But she heard a strange voice.

It was a man's voice, loud and hearty. It said, "Get a move on, Manzo. Let's get this load in. It's coming night after awhile."

Another voice drawled lazily, "Aw-aw, Roy!"

Close together, Laura and Carrie looked out from the edge of the standing grass. The hayfield was not Pa's hayfield. A strange wagon stood there and on its rack was an enormous load of hay. On the high top of that load, up against the blinding sky, a boy was lying. He lay on his stomach, his chin on his hands and his feet in the air.

The strange man lifted up a huge forkful of hay and pitched it onto the boy. It buried him and he scrambled up out of it, laughing and shaking hay off his head and his shoulders. He had black hair and blue eyes and his face and his arms were sun-burned brown.

He stood up on the high load of hay against the sky and saw Laura. He said, "Hello there!" They both stood watching Laura and Carrie come out of the tall standing grass—like rabbits, Laura thought. She wanted to turn and run back into hiding.

"I thought Pa was here," she said, while Carrie stood small and still behind her.

The man said, "We haven't seen anybody around here. Who is your Pa?" The boy told him, "Mr. Ingalls. Isn't he?" he asked Laura. He was still looking at her.

"Yes," she said, and she looked at the horses hitched to the wagon. She had seen those beautiful brown horses before, their haunches gleaming in the sun and the black manes glossy on their glossy necks. They were the Wilder boys' horses. The man and the boy must be the Wilder brothers.

"I can see him from here. He's just over there," the boy said. Laura looked up and saw him pointing. His blue eyes twinkled down at her as if he had known her a long time.

"Thank you," Laura said primly and she and Carrie walked away, along the road that the Morgan team and the wagon had broken through the slough grass.

"Whoa!" Pa said when he saw them. "Whew!" he said, taking off his hat and wiping the sweat from his forehead.

Laura gave him the mowing-machine section, and she and Carrie watched while he opened the tool-box, took the cutter-bar from the machine, and knocked out the broken section. He set the new one in its place and hammered down the rivets to hold it. "There!" he said. "Tell your Ma I'll be late for supper. I'm going to finish cutting this piece."

The mowing machine was humming steadily when Laura and Carrie went on toward the shanty.

"Were you much scared, Laura?" Carrie asked.

"Well, some, but all's well that ends well," Laura said.

"It was my fault. I wanted to go that way," said Carrie.

"It was my fault because I'm older," Laura said. "But we've learned a lesson. I guess we'll stay on the road after this."

"Are you going to tell Ma and Pa?" Carrie timidly asked.

"We have to if they ask us," said Laura.

thinking about it

1 Lost! Nearly everyone has been lost sometime. Remember one of your "lost" experiences. How was it like the experience of Laura and Carrie?

2 Find the scene where Laura and Carrie are lost in the slough. How can you read this scene so that people can see it, hear it, and feel it? Demonstrate.

3 You are making a silent movie or video of this selection. Plan or show the most gripping scene and the happiest scene.

More Books About Laura and Her Family
Altogether there are nine "Little House" books. Do you have a particular favorite?

Samuel's

Choice

by Richard Berleth
illustrated by James Watling

My master, Isaac van Ditmas, was a very rich farmer. In my fourteenth year, he bought me from his old aunt in Flushing and took me from my parents to work as a slave in his flour mill on Gowanus Creek in Brooklyn. That same time he bought Sana Williams, Toby, and others to keep the gardens and kitchen of his big house on New York Harbor.

At the end of Long Island, the Heights of Brooklyn overlooked the East River and Manhattan Island. To the south lay the town of Brooklyn; it was only a small one in those days. The long South Road ran across Long Island's hills, through fields of wheat and rye, connecting Brooklyn town with the Narrows at the entrance to New York Harbor.

Gowanus Creek, where the flour mill stood,

wound out of this harbor into the green fields and lost itself in ponds and marshes. On a summer evening, the mosquitoes rose like clouds from still waters and settled, stinging, on our bare arms and necks.

Farmer Isaac was a strict man. Our day began at sunrise and ended when the light faded. Round and round the great stone wheel rolled and rumbled all day long, driven by tides flowing in and out of the creek. We ground wheat to make bread at the mill. We shoveled the flour into bags, and loaded the bags into boats, to be brought to bakers in Manhattan. But little bread we ever saw. Van Ditmas was a stingy man. Many nights I went to bed with my stomach growling and only the taste of the raw flour on my lips.

When Farmer Isaac saw that I had grown strong and could row a boat well, he taught me about the currents that flow between Brooklyn and Manhattan, about setting a sail and holding a course. I was to row Mrs. van Ditmas and her daughters over to Manhattan, or down the Brooklyn shore to Staten Island across the harbor. Isaac shook me by the collar and warned me never to row or sail except where he sent me. I was his property, according to the laws of the Crown Colony, and he could do what he wanted with me.

Work you do not choose to do is always tiring. And even the house slaves, who labored in Farmer Isaac's kitchen, got little sleep and less food. Whenever I felt the fresh sea breeze on my face, I would look up at the gulls flying where they pleased

and I would dream. I wondered how it was to be free like them, to go where I wanted.

America, being ruled by the king of England, was not a separate country. And these were troubled times in all the colonies. The night came when Manhattan Island was lit up like daytime with a hundred bonfires. We gathered on the steps of the great house and heard the cheers and shouts echo over the water. Then came the sound of drums and fifes, songs and cannon firing.

"What's all that racket over there?" Sana asked.

"That's the sound of people going free," old Toby

answered. "Free from the king of England. Free from the likes of van Ditmas."

"How they get free, Toby?"

"Why they up and said they was free, girl, and wrote those words down on paper."

Sana laughed. "You gotta do more than say you're free. That king and Isaac, do they care what anybody say?"

What was it, I wondered, that made people think they could change their lives? They called their freedom "liberty," and they marched through Brooklyn town cheering for that liberty.

When the Sons of Liberty finally came, waving their flags, Isaac locked us in the house.

In the kitchen, the servants argued. "Liberty ain't for Africans," one said. "And it got nothin' to do with us," another said.

But Sana just shook her head. She was fifteen and had been to church school. She could write her name and could read. "Nobody here's gonna be free unless they take the risk. Open your eyes! War is coming to Brooklyn 'tween that English king and those Sons of Liberty. We can't say who'll win. We can't say how many black slaves are ever gonna get free. But one thing is sure—it's never gonna happen under Isaac van Ditmas."

The talk made my head spin. One moment it seemed to offer hope, and then the arguments turned and I didn't feel hope anymore. One day Liberty men nailed a proclamation to a tree by the South Road. But before anyone could tell me what it said, Isaac came and tore it down and stamped on it in the dust. That was the day Sana promised she would teach me to read. "That writing, Samuel," she said later, "was the Declaration of Independence, made by Thomas Jefferson in the Congress at Philadelphia."

So the summer of 1776, my fourteenth one, passed on. Day by day, my back and arms grew stronger with hard work. More than once I looked up from filling flour sacks to find a cool jar of buttermilk left by Sana. Then I'd drink the milk and fill the empty jar with flour. When she fetched the jar back, she would hide it. One day I asked what she wanted with so much flour. She just smiled and said, "That flour will be bread for our freedom day."

While I sailed on Farmer Isaac's errands or loaded sacks of flour, the war crept towards Brooklyn. On a fine morning we woke in the slave quarters to the thunder of great guns out in the harbor. I ran up to the house. Sana just kept on calmly with her work. "Washington's come to New York," she said, grinning. "Those are guns out of Governors Island practicing to scare off the British."

Well, the guns sure scared off Farmer Isaac. After Washington arrived, he and Mrs. van Ditmas never crossed to Manhattan again. I hoisted the sail of my boat to carry the farmer's wife and daughters, with all their trunks, to an old uncle's house on Staten Island.

And there on Staten Island, I saw them. The king's army had come from across the sea and on the hillside meadows had pitched its tents by the thousands. The sun glinted on rows of brass cannon and bayonets. Redcoats came down from the hills. They spread over the green grass like streams of blood, and they sat in barges and were rowed across to the Brooklyn shore. A barge passed nearby. We saw the smiling, sunburned faces of the soldiers. "Hurrah!" they cheered, and the van Ditmas girls waved and giggled.

C·26

Back in the kitchen of the big house, I told what I had seen.

"Those great ships have hundreds of cannon," Toby said.

"There's got to be thousands of Redcoats," somebody else said, "and they gonna whip these Liberty Boys but good."

"General Washington will find a way," Sana said, but her eyes held back tears. "It can't just end like this!"

Old Toby put an arm around her. "Trouble is, dear, it can. These Americans are settin' up to fight their king, and that means all the king's ships, and men, and cannon."

"No business for us black slaves, I'm tellin' you," said Joseph Martin.

"Not with Isaac down so hard on the Liberty Boys," Loretta added.

It seemed to me the slaves were right. I could not think how the ordinary Americans I had seen, fresh from their farms and shops, could ever drive away an army of real soldiers.

The next day, while I loaded sacks into a wagon, I heard the sound of fifes and drums. Southwards, along the road past the mill, came a hundred of Washington's recruits, their feet shuffling in the dust. An American officer rode beside them on a gray farmhorse.

"Captain!" Sana called to him. "Thousands of them are landing down the shore!"

"We know that, girl," he called back. "Don't worry, we'll handle them lobster backs. General Washington himself is coming over to Brooklyn." But the men marching past us didn't look so sure. Many seemed frightened. Some were barefoot. Some looked hungry and sick. Their flags drooped. As they passed, Sana read the names of the colonies embroidered on their banners: Pennsylvania, Delaware, Maryland, Rhode Island. They had come from far away to a strange place.

Farmer Isaac stood by the fence, puffing on his pipe. "You be quiet, girl. This isn't no fight of yours. If them fools want to break the king's law, they can get themselves killed with no help from my slaves."

Sana shook her head. I knew she felt sorry for the ragged men and boys marching past. Maybe they were not fighting for her liberty. Not yet. But freedom had to start somewhere. That summer it was starting in Brooklyn.

When the officer was gone, and Isaac, too, one of his men stopped by the wagon. He just stood there and stared at me.

"You thirsty?" I asked him. He nodded and held his empty canteen upside down. I snatched my jug of buttermilk out of the wagon and poured it into the canteen. The boy took a long drink.

"Thanks," he said. "My name's Nathaniel. Joined up at Boston on my fourteenth birthday."

"You know how to shoot that thing?" I asked, pointing at his musket.

"Think so," he muttered. "Shot it yesterday in camp."

"You scared?" I asked him.

"No, I ain't," he said.

"Well, you oughta be," I told him.

All day long the guns crashed and boomed on the Long Island hills. While the mill wheel rumbled and ground, soldiers rushed down the South Road.

Suddenly there was shouting. A soldier appeared in the doorway. "The British are coming!" he cried. "The Americans are running!"

The road filled with crowds of American soldiers, now running north along the road, back toward Washington's lines. Tired, frightened people. Most were sopping wet. Where they stopped to rest, the dust turned to mud under their feet.

Cannonballs were whizzing through the air. One crashed through the roof of the mill. Farmer Isaac was nowhere to be seen. Sana knelt by someone who had fallen beside the road. She tied a strip of petticoat around a bloody gash in his leg. He was soaked and shaking. When I looked at his face, I saw that he was Nathaniel, the boy with the empty canteen.

"Stop staring," Sana shouted at me. "He's trembling. Wrap him in them empty sacks." Nathaniel told us how he swam across Gowanus Creek to escape from the British. But the tide was rising fast. Dozens of Americans were wounded and many couldn't swim.

The army was trapped without boats in the swamps around the creek. Some were still fighting, but lots of soldiers were being shot like ducks in the marshes. Washington's men needed help badly.

Sana's eyes pleaded with me. She knew I tied my boat in the reeds along the creek. Her look said, "It's up to you, Samuel."

Nathaniel groaned. The small red spot on his bandage had begun to spread. Toby had come and was kneeling beside Sana. He shrugged. "You got the boat, Samuel. It's your choice."

Sana and Toby got set to carry Nathaniel up the road into the American lines. Sana caught me looking at the bag on her shoulder.

"That's my freedom flour," she said. "I'm going where I can bake my freedom loaf." A moment later, more soldiers ran between us. When they had passed, Sana, Toby, and Nathaniel were gone.

All at once the road was empty. From away in the distance came the roar of muskets. Isaac van Ditmas was gone. Sana was gone and the soldiers were, too. I was alone.

Was this freedom? I thought about that boy Nathaniel from far away. How a lot more people just like him were trapped in the marshes along the creek. And how Isaac sneered at them, and how the British king from across the waters sent his soldiers to shoot and imprison them. I looked at my hands, grown strong from pulling ropes and oars and sacks. Then I

knew my choice. Those hands now were going to pull people, pull them to freedom.

I ran to the creek, pushed the boat out into the rushing tide, and slid the oars into their locks. On the opposite bank Americans were wading in the muddy water up to their waists, shouting for help. In the distance others were holding the British back from the water's edge. Great clouds of gunsmoke rolled over these brave soldiers. When the air cleared, I could see fewer and fewer of them.

As I pulled near, wet and weary men flopped into

the boat. Others clung to the sides. "Row, row!" they shouted. I pulled on the oars with all my might. Out we shot into the current. Bullets splashed in the water near us. When we reached the far bank, the men cheered. I turned again into the creek and rowed back for more.

Six times I crossed the creek. Each time the battle grew closer, the fleeing Americans fewer. By now muddy water slopped around my ankles. My back ached from pulling on the oars.

Just as I was raising the sail to race out of the creek,

I glimpsed a big man in a blue coat and three-cornered hat alone in the bullreeds. He threw himself into the boat and ordered me to sail for Washington's camp. The British were close behind him. As we fled down the creek into New York Harbor, they fired at us from the banks. When the big man had caught his breath, he pointed up at the sail. Black holes gaped in the canvas.

"Musket balls," he said and winked. "Compliments of General Cornwallis."

As the boat carried us out into the harbor, I steered northward along the Brooklyn shore toward Brooklyn Heights and Washington's camp. I wondered what Farmer Isaac would say about his torn sail. But most of all, I wondered what had happened to Sana and Toby.

My passenger's name was Major Mordecai Gist. He commanded the Maryland soldiers who had held back the British while other Americans escaped. "Oh, what brave boys I lost today," said Major Gist, "and this war has only begun." He asked how I came to be fishing men out of the creek. I told him about Farmer Isaac, Sana, and Nathaniel.

When I tied the boat to the dock below the Heights, Major Gist clapped his hands on my shoulders and looked me in the eyes. "Samuel," he said, "out in that creek you did more than many a free man for your country. I'd take it as a privilege if you'd consent to be my orderly and march beside me. And General Washington may need handy boatmen like you soon enough."

The next day it rained and rained. A thick sea fog covered the land. I looked everywhere for Sana. Many soldiers crowded into the camp, but they could tell me nothing. Alone and frightened, I mended the holes in my sail, pushing the big needle through the canvas, drawing it back again. Then, I heard voices nearby.

Major Gist stood there with an officer in a fine blue uniform. They asked me how deep the water was at this point between Brooklyn and Manhattan. They wanted to know if a British ship could sail between the two places. I told them that most ships could. Only the fog was keeping the British men-of-war from trapping Washington's army on Long Island.

The officer in the blue uniform thanked me. He and Major Gist walked away, looking thoughtful.

The next day the heavy rains continued. I spread the sail over the boat and slept snug and dry. Then I heard the voice I missed more than any in the world calling, "Samuel, Samuel Abraham!" Sana had found me! It was not a dream. "You chose, Samuel," she said. "You did it right. You chose our new country." From under her cloak she took a hot, steaming loaf wrapped in a napkin—her freedom bread, the sweetest I ever tasted. While we ate, she told me that Toby and Nathaniel were safe.

But this new country was in danger. Major Gist came to me again and explained that every boat was needed to carry Washington's army from Brooklyn to Manhattan. The army had to retreat that night. I was going to help save the army with Farmer Isaac's boat. Wouldn't he be surprised?

On the night that General Washington's army left Brooklyn, the worst storm I'd ever seen blew in from the Northeast. The wind howled. It drove the rain, stinging, into our eyes. It shook buildings and knocked down chimneys. And it whipped the water at Brooklyn Ferry into a sea of foam.

Down from the Heights in file marched Washington's army. The men entered the boats Major Gist and others had gathered at the ferry landing.

"What we need is a rope to cling to," someone said in the dark. "A rope stretching from here to Manhattan to guide us against the wind and current."

"There's rope here in the shipyard," a soldier remembered. "Buoys to float the rope across, too. But who can cross this flood in the dark?"

"Can you do it, Samuel?" Major Gist asked. "Can you get across with the rope?"

"I can do it, Major," I shouted, the wind tearing the words out of my mouth. But I wasn't sure. Even if the rope were fed out from shore slowly, the sail might split or the rope might tear down the mast. But the British ships were sure to force their way between Brooklyn and Manhattan. I had to try.

When the rope was ready, I tied it to the foot of the mast. Sana jumped into the boat. I shouted at her to stay behind, but she wouldn't move. There was no time to lose. I shoved off into the swirling current.

My only hope was to let the shore current carry me out into midstream, and then, as the wind and tide thrust the boat toward the other shore, raise the sail and race for the Manhattan landing.

Fighting the rudder, I heard Sana's voice in my ear. "Will we make it, Samuel?" Water crashed over the side. Sana was bailing as fast as she could. "I can't swim, Samuel!" she cried into the wind. We were halfway across to Manhattan, and the boat was filling with sea. The gale was spinning us around. The rope was pulling us backward. I heaved at the sail, praying the mending wouldn't tear.

Then, as the sail filled, the boom swung around with a crack, and we were darting forward at last. On the Manhattan landing, by lantern light, we could see people waiting. Over the roar of the storm, we heard them cheering us on. But Isaac's boat was sinking. The rope was tearing the mast out of the bottom. With a terrible crash, the mast broke and was carried over the side. A second later the bow smashed into the side of a wharf, and I found myself in the water swimming with one arm, clinging to Sana with the other.

We stumbled ashore on Manhattan Island, where kind people wrapped us in blankets. They were smiling—the rope was across! The boats full of Washington's soldiers would follow. We had done it, together.

All through the night Washington's men followed that rope, boat after boat, across the water. In the stormy darkness, every soldier escaped from Long Island.

And so the fight for freedom would go on. It would take many long years before we would beat the British king, but never again did I wonder what freedom was, or what it cost. It was people pulling together. It was strong hands helping. It was one person caring about another.

And where was Washington? Many times that night Sana and I hoped to see him.

"Why, Samuel," Major Gist told us later, "he was that officer in the blue coat who asked you how deep the water was between Brooklyn and Manhattan. Last night the general arrested a farmer in Brooklyn for helping the British. That farmer, Isaac van Ditmas, turned all of his property over to the Army of the Continental Congress in exchange for his freedom. It seems now that you and Sana have no master."

From that day forward, we and Isaac's other slaves were to be citizens of a new nation.

C·39

HISTORICAL NOTE: The Battle of Long Island was George Washington's first battle in the American War for Independence. It was a defeat. From Brooklyn, General Washington retreated to Manhattan, then to New Jersey, and in the last month of 1776, he crossed the Delaware River into Pennsylvania. Thus ended one of the longer and more bitter retreats in American history. On the day after Christmas, Washington crossed the icy Delaware once more into New Jersey. There, at Trenton and again at Princeton, his soldiers (many of whom had escaped from Brooklyn) defeated their enemy. In 1781, General Cornwallis finally surrendered at Yorktown. The British troops who fired on Samuel at Gowanus Creek on August 27, 1776, were commanded by General Cornwallis.

Major Mordecai Gist led the Maryland state troops in the Battle of Long Island. He and Isaac van Ditmas are historical figures (although the arrest of van Ditmas did not actually occur). Samuel Abraham and Sana Williams are fictional, but modeled on the many nameless people of Brooklyn, slave and free, who made Washington's escape possible.

thinking about it

1 A story can pick you up and plop you down in a dangerous part of the world in 1776. If you had to pick two scenes to be dropped into, which ones would they be?

2 You are trying to convince someone that she or he should try reading historical fiction. Use *Samuel's Choice* as your example. Find which part you'll recommend and show how you'll recommend it.

3 A newly invented "time-travel phone" has been rigged up to let you talk to Samuel. You have exactly three minutes to tell him what he ought to know. That isn't very much time to tell him over two hundred years of history, so plan what you'll say.

*The presidential candidate, June 1860. Of this
photograph Lincoln said, "That looks better and
expresses me better than any I have ever seen;
if it pleases the people, I am satisfied."*

The Mysterious Mr. Lincoln

RUSSELL FREEDMAN

*"If any personal description of me is
thought desirable, it may be said, I am,
in height, six feet, four inches, nearly;
lean in flesh, weighing, on average,
one hundred and eighty pounds; dark
complexion, with coarse black hair
and grey eyes—no other marks or
brands recollected."*

Abraham Lincoln wasn't the sort of man who could
lose himself in a crowd. After all, he stood six
feet four inches tall, and to top it off, he wore a high
silk hat.

His height was mostly in his long bony legs. When
he sat in a chair, he seemed no taller than anyone
else. It was only when he stood up that he towered
above other men.

At first glance, most people thought he was homely.
Lincoln thought so too, referring once to his "poor,
lean, lank face." As a young man he was sensitive
about his gawky looks, but in time, he learned to
laugh at himself. When a rival called him "two-faced"
during a political debate, Lincoln replied: "I leave it to
my audience. If I had another face, do you think I'd
wear this one?"

According to those who knew him, Lincoln was a man of many faces. In repose, he often seemed sad and gloomy. But when he began to speak, his expression changed. "The dull, listless features dropped like a mask," said a Chicago newspaperman. "The eyes began to sparkle, the mouth to smile, the whole countenance was wreathed in animation, so that a stranger would have said, 'Why, this man, so angular and solemn a moment ago, is really handsome!'"

Lincoln was the most photographed man of his time, but his friends insisted that no photo ever did him justice. It's no wonder. Back then, cameras required long exposures. The person being photographed had to "freeze" as the seconds ticked by. If he blinked an eye, the picture would be blurred. That's why Lincoln looks so stiff and formal in his photos. We never see him laughing or joking.

Artists and writers tried to capture the "real" Lincoln that the camera missed, but something about the man always escaped them. His changeable features, his tones, gestures, and expressions, seemed to defy description.

Today it's hard to imagine Lincoln as he really was. And he never cared to reveal much about himself. In company he was witty and talkative, but he rarely betrayed his inner feelings. According to William Herndon, his law partner, he was "the most secretive—reticent—shut-mouthed man that ever lived."

In his own time, Lincoln was never fully understood even by his closest friends. Since then, his life story has

Wearing his familiar stovepipe hat, Lincoln towers above General George B. McClellan and other army officers during a visit to McClellan's battlefield headquarters near Antietam, Maryland, October 3, 1862.

been told and retold so many times, he has become as much a legend as a flesh-and-blood human being. While the legend is based on truth, it is only partly true. And it hides the man behind it like a disguise.

The legendary Lincoln is known as Honest Abe, a humble man of the people who rose from a log cabin to the White House. There's no doubt that Lincoln was a poor boy who made good. And it's true that he carried his folksy manners and homespun speech to the White House with him. He said "howdy" to visitors and invited them to "stay a spell." He greeted diplomats while wearing carpet slippers, called his wife "mother" at receptions, and told bawdy jokes at cabinet meetings.

From a log cabin to the White House. A replica of Lincoln's Kentucky birthplace.

Lincoln may have seemed like a common man, but he wasn't. His friends agreed that he was one of the most ambitious people they had ever known. Lincoln struggled hard to rise above his log-cabin origins, and he was proud of his achievements. By the time he ran for president he was a wealthy man, earning a large income from his law practice and his many investments. As for the nickname Abe, he hated it. No one who knew him well ever called him Abe to his face. They addressed him as Lincoln or Mr. Lincoln.

Lincoln is often described as a sloppy dresser, careless about his appearance. In fact, he patronized the best tailor in Springfield, Illinois, buying two suits a year. That was at a time when many men lived, died, and were buried in the same suit.

It's true that Lincoln had little formal "eddication," as he would have pronounced it. Almost everything he "larned" he taught himself. All his life he said "thar" for *there,* "git" for *get,* "kin" for *can.* Even so, he became an eloquent public speaker who could hold a vast audience spellbound, and a great writer whose finest phrases still ring in our ears. He was known to sit up late into the night, discussing Shakespeare's plays with White House visitors.

He was certainly a humorous man, famous for his rollicking stories. But he was also moody and melancholy, tormented by long and frequent bouts of depression. Humor was his therapy. He relied on his yarns, a friend observed, to "whistle down sadness."

He had a cool, logical mind, trained in the courtroom, and a practical, commonsense approach to problems. Yet he was deeply superstitious, a believer in dreams, omens, and visions.

We admire Lincoln today as an American folk hero. During the Civil War, however, he was the most unpopular president the nation had ever known. His critics called him a tyrant, a hick, a stupid baboon who was unfit for his office. As commander in chief of the armed forces, he was denounced as a bungling amateur who meddled in military affairs he knew nothing about. But he also had his supporters. They praised him as a farsighted statesman, a military mastermind who engineered the Union victory.

Lincoln is best known as the Great Emancipator, the man who freed the slaves. Yet he did not enter the war with that idea in mind. "My paramount object in this struggle *is* to save the Union," he said in 1862, "and is *not* either to save or destroy slavery." As the war continued, Lincoln's attitude changed. Eventually he came to regard the conflict as a moral crusade to wipe out the sin of slavery.

No black leader was more critical of Lincoln than the fiery abolitionist writer and editor Frederick Douglass. Douglass had grown up as a slave. He had won his freedom by escaping to the North. Early in the war, impatient with Lincoln's cautious leadership, Douglass called him "preeminently the white man's president, entirely devoted to the welfare of white men." Later, Douglass changed his mind and came to admire Lincoln. Several years after the war, he said this about the sixteenth president:

"His greatest mission was to accomplish two things: first, to save his country from dismemberment and ruin; and, second, to free his country from the great crime of slavery. . . . taking him for all in all, measuring the tremendous magnitude of the work before him, considering the necessary means to ends, and surveying the end from the beginning, infinite wisdom has seldom sent any man into the world better fitted for his mission than Abraham Lincoln."

1861.

1862.

1863.

1864.

The strain of war. A sampling of photographs taken during Lincoln's four years in office shows how the pressures and anxieties of the war became etched in his face.

Looking for the Man Behind the Myth

by Russell Freedman

Russell Freedman

I've never forgotten the framed photograph of Abraham Lincoln that hung just outside Mrs. Koeppe's office at the grammar school I attended in San Francisco. Mrs. Koeppe was our principal. When I was summoned to her office, I would wait nervously outside and stare at the pendulum clock tick-tick-ticking on one wall, and at the bearded face of Abraham Lincoln gazing down at me from another. Honest Abe always seemed to know when I was in trouble.

My schoolbooks told me that our sixteenth president had freed the slaves and led the Union through the Civil War. I understood that Lincoln was important, but somehow he just didn't seem real to me. I thought of him as that imposing marble statue at the Lincoln Memorial in Washington,

D.C.—bigger than life but cold to the touch, not really human.

It wasn't until years later that something I happened to read ignited my interest in Lincoln. I read that he was depressed sometimes, and that he didn't always make decisions easily. Abraham Lincoln *depressed?* The Great Emancipator *indecisive?* Curious, I began to read more about him. I discovered that a complex and fascinating human being was hidden behind the historical make up. That's when I decided to write about the real Lincoln, warts and all.

I spent several months researching my biography before I actually began writing. I read a great many books about Lincoln, of course, and I also had a chance to enjoy some on-the-spot, eye-witness research. I

Like most boys of his time, Russell Freedman loved to pretend to be a cowboy.

followed the Lincoln Trail all the way from his log-cabin birthplace in Kentucky to Ford's Theatre in Washington, where the President was shot, and the rooming house across the street, where he died the following morning.

Some of my research time was spent looking for historical photographs.

Old photos are important in my books because they bring the past to life in a way that nothing else can. I always do my own photo research, since I'm the only one who knows exactly what I'm looking for. But I do it with the expert help of librarians who specialize in photographic archives. For my Lincoln biography, I searched through the archives at the Illinois State Historical Library in Springfield, at the Chicago Historical Society, and at the Library of Congress and the National Archives in Washington.

Along with photos of Lincoln, his family and friends, the Civil War, and so on, I looked at newspapers and magazines, at posters, and at other documents of the period. I included photos of some of those documents in my book—Lincoln's marriage license, for example; a wanted poster for a runaway slave; and a handwritten copy of the Gettysburg Address.

Ideally, the photos in a book should reveal something that words alone cannot express. And the words, in turn, should say something that isn't evident in the photos. No words could possibly capture the careworn expression on Lincoln's face during his final days as president, when the Civil War, the bloodiest war in American history, was at last coming to an end. Lincoln agonized over every casualty. Looking at the photos taken of the president at that time, you can see how the worries and anxieties of the war became etched into his face. Those photographs speak for themselves.

thinking about it

1 Close your eyes. Can you see Lincoln? Listen. Can you hear him? Can you see him move? These are experiences biographers may have as they study the person they are writing about. These are also experiences a reader of biography may have. Tell your experience while reading about Lincoln.

2 Russell Freedman writes, "I decided to write about the real Lincoln, warts and all." Find examples of "warts" in the Lincoln biography. How do they help you understand the man?

3 Try as you might, you can never read all the biographies published. So how will you choose? First, figure out whom you wish to read about and why. Second, decide on your standards: what you should find in a well-presented biography. Plan now. Whom will you read about? What standards will you set?

A Cow Herder
on Horseback

RUSSELL FREEDMAN

**I've roamed the Texas prairies,
I've followed the cattle trail;
I've rid a pitchin' pony
Till the hair come off his tail.**[©]

ACENTURY AGO, in the years following the Civil War, one million mustang ponies and ten million head of longhorn cattle were driven north out of Texas. Bawling and bellowing, the lanky longhorns tramped along dusty trails in herds that numbered a thousand animals or more.

Behind and beside and ahead of each herd rode groups of men on horseback. Often, they sang to the cattle as they drove them on. These old-time cow herders were mostly very young men, and in time they came to be known as cowboys.

Some were boys in fact as well as name. Youngsters still in their teens commonly worked as horse wranglers, caring for the saddle ponies that traveled with every trail outfit. A typical trail-driving cowboy was in his early twenties. Except for some cooks and bosses, there were few thirty-year-old men on the trail.

Cowboys drove great herds across wild prairies from Texas to markets in Kansas and beyond. They

These cowboys drove a herd of longhorns from Texas to Montana during the late 1880s. In Miles City, Montana, they went to a photographer's studio and posed proudly for this group portrait.

swam the cattle across rivers and stayed with them during stampedes. A man spent eighteen hours a day in the saddle. At night he slept on the ground. Sometimes he lived on the trail for months with no comforts but a campfire and his bedroll.

At the end of the drive, the cattle were sold, the hands were paid off, and the trail outfit split up. Then the cowboys went into town to scrape off the trail dust and celebrate. Usually they stopped at the pineboard photographer's studio found in nearly every western cattle town. Decked out in their best duds and sporting the tools of their trade, they posed proudly for souvenir pictures to send to the folks back home. Some of those old photographs still survive. In them we can glimpse the cowboy as he really was, a hundred years ago.

The cowboy trade goes back more than four hundred years. It began in Mexico during the sixteenth century, when Spanish settlers brought the first domesticated horses and cattle to North America. Back home, the Spanish had kept their cattle penned up in pastures. But in the wide-open spaces of the New World, the cattle were allowed to wander freely, finding their own grass and water. The animals flourished. Soon, huge Spanish ranches were scattered across northern Mexico.

Since the cattle roamed far and wide, the ranchers needed skilled horsemen to look after their herds. They began to teach the local Indians to ride horses and handle cattle on the open range. These barefoot

Indian cow herders were called *vaqueros,* from the Spanish word *vaca,* for cow. They were the first true cowboys, and they spent their days from sunrise to sunset in the saddle. They became experts at snaring a running steer with a braided rawhide rope, called *la reata* in Spanish. Over the years *la reata*—the lariat—became the cowboy's most important tool, and the Mexican vaquero became a proud and independent ranch hand.

Vaqueros drove the first herds of cattle north into Texas early in the eighteenth century. By the time of the American Civil War (1861–1865), millions of hardy long-horned cattle were roaming the Texas plains. Many of these animals were descended from strays and runaways that had escaped from their owners, and they were as wild as buffalo or deer. They clustered together in small herds, hiding in thickets by day, running by night. If anyone tried to approach them on foot, they would paw the earth and toss their heads in anger.

Like most of the South, Texas was poor

A Spanish vaquero

when the Civil War ended. Confederate money no longer had any value. The state's economy was in ruins. Yet longhorns were running wild all over the state.

Before the war, cattle had been raised mainly for their hides (for leather) and tallow, or fat (for candles and soap). Now, new methods of meat-packing and refrigeration had created a profitable market for beef in the crowded cities of the North. Texas had plenty of beef on the hoof, but there were no railroads linking Texas with the rest of the country, where the beef was in demand. The only way to get the cattle to market was to walk them hundreds of miles north to the nearest railroad.

As Texas farmers and ranchers came home from the war, they began to organize what they called "cow hunts." By capturing wild longhorns and branding them as his own, a rancher could build up his herds and drive them north to be sold. Cow-hunters used the same methods to catch wild cattle that Mexican vaqueros had been using for a long time. They found a herd of longhorns by moonlight and fired a gun to make them stampede. Riding with the herd, they let the longhorns run for hours, until the cattle grew tired and slowed to a trot or walk. Then the men kept the animals moving for the next day or so, until the longhorns were so hungry and exhausted, they had tamed down and could be handled with ease.

Once the cattle had been caught and branded, they were set loose to graze until they were ready for market. Then they were rounded up and driven in large herds to Kansas railroad towns, where they were loaded aboard freight cars and shipped to meat-packing plants in Kansas City and Chicago.

As the demand for beef grew, the cattle-raising industry spread northward from Texas. New ranches began to spring up all across the northern plains, where only a few years before herds of buffalo had grazed. By the 1870s, most of the buffalo had been slaughtered. They were replaced by longhorn cattle brought up the trails from Texas. Soon, a vast tract of cattle country stretched from Colorado up through Wyoming, Montana, and the Dakotas.

At the heart of this booming cattle industry was the hard-working cowboy. Who was he, where was he from, and what was he like?

To begin with, most cowboys were Texans and other southerners, discharged soldiers back from the war. Jobs were scarce in the South, and the prospering cattle ranchers needed plenty of new hands. Along with the southerners, there were a number of mustered-out Union soldiers. Eventually, men and boys from many backgrounds and all parts of the country began to arrive in Texas, seeking jobs as cowhands. Some had been unlucky at home and were looking for a fresh start. Others were drawn to Texas because they had heard that a cowboy's life was adventurous and exciting.

Today, in movies and TV shows about the Old West, cowboys are usually white. In real life, they were often black or Mexican. Texas had been a slaveholding state before the Civil War. On Texas ranches, slaves broke horses and herded cattle. When the war ended, many freed slaves from Texas and other southern states went to work as professional cowhands. Most Texas trail outfits included black cowboys, and a few outfits were all black.

Mexican cowhands, descendants of the vaqueros, were common in southern Texas, where many ranches were still owned by old Spanish families. Other cowboys were American Indians, or had some Indian blood. In the Indian Territory (now Oklahoma), a number of cattle ranches were operated entirely by Native American cowboys.

In the movies, cowboys seem to spend a good part of their time chasing outlaws, battling Indians, rescuing the rancher's daughter, and hanging out in

Cowboys at mealtime, photographed in the Texas Panhandle around 1885. Black cowboys were a part of most Texas trail outfits.

riotous cow towns like Abilene and Dodge City. They wear huge white hats, skintight shirts, and shiny six-shooters slung low on each hip. That's not quite the way it was in the real Wild West.

A real cowboy was paid to herd cows. He spent most of his time rounding up longhorns, branding calves, and driving the herds to market. He was lucky if he made it into town twice in one year. Out on the range he wore practical work clothing, rode a horse owned by his employer, and seldom carried a gun. When he did, he wore it high and snug around his waist. He never carried two guns.

"There is one thing I would like to get straight," recalled an old-time cowboy named Teddy Blue Abbott. "I punched cows from '71 on [when he was ten years old], and I never yet saw a cowboy with two guns. I mean two six-shooters. Wild Bill carried two guns and so did some of those other city marshals, like Bat Masterson, but they were professional gunmen themselves, not cowpunchers. . . . A cowboy with two guns is all movie stuff, and so is this business of a gun on each hip."

Most cowboys were not sharpshooters, yet their work demanded exceptional skills. A cowboy had to be an expert roper and rider, an artist at busting broncs and whacking bulls. He had to know how to doctor an ailing cow or find a lost calf, how to calm a restless herd in the middle of the night, how to head off a thousand stampeding longhorns.

On a ranch, he worked ten to fourteen hours a day. On trail drives, he herded cattle from before dawn to after dusk, then spent two more hours on night guard duty. He had a tough, dirty, sweaty job, and often a dangerous one. He might be kicked by a horse, charged by a steer, trampled in a stampede, drowned during a river crossing, or caught on the open prairie in the midst of an electrical storm. Probably more cowboys were killed by lightning than by outlaws or Indians. Riding accidents were the most common cause of cowboy deaths, followed by pneumonia.

Teddy Blue Abbott went up the trail for the first time in 1879, when he was eighteen years old. Sixty years later he recalled the men he had worked with: "In person the cowboys were mostly medium-sized men, as a heavy man was hard on horses, quick and wiry, and as a rule very good natured; in fact, it did not pay to be anything else. In character, their like never was or will be again. They were intensely loyal to the outfit they were working for and would fight to the death for it. They would follow their wagon boss through hell and never complain. I have seen them ride into camp after two days and nights on herd, lay down their saddle blankets in the rain and sleep like dead men, then get up laughing and joking about some good time they had in Ogallala or Dodge City. Living that kind of life, they were bound to be wild and brave."

thinking about it

1 Teddy Blue Abbott is a real cowboy, and Wild Tom Two-Guns is a movie cowboy. They're having a showdown. Each wants to set the record straight. What do they argue about when they discuss cowboys from the Wild West?

2 Authors can't tell everything. There isn't space, and sometimes there isn't information either. After reading "A Cow Herder on Horseback," think of three more things you'd like to know about cowboys.

3 Think of a 1990s job that is similar to the work of a cowboy. How is the job the same? How is it different?

Another Book by Russell Freedman
The spectacular story of man's first flight is told in *The Wright Brothers: How They Invented the Airplane.*

Hector

by Joan Hewett – photographs by Richard Hewett

Ten-year-old Hector Almaraz is a Mexican American. For as long as he can remember he has lived in Los Angeles—in this neighborhood, on this block.

Hector's parents are Leopoldo and Rosario Almaraz. He also has three brothers: nine-year-old Polo, and Miguel and Ernesto, who are seven and four.

Hector and Polo were born in Guadalajara, Mexico, and are Mexican citizens, like their parents. Their younger brothers, Miguel and Ernesto, were born in Los Angeles and are American citizens.

When Hector's parents came to California to find work, they did not understand English. But they had heard so much about Los Angeles, from sisters and brothers and their own parents, that the city seemed almost familiar.

At first they stayed with relatives. Then Leopoldo found a job, and the family moved to Eagle Rock, a residential section of the city.

They are still there. The streets and parks are safe, and an elementary school and a Catholic church are only a few blocks from their small, bungalow-style apartment.

Hector has lots of friends. Most of them live on his block. They play together after school and on Saturdays and Sundays.

Soccer is one of their favorite games. So is baseball. When it is baseball season, they dig out a bat, ball, and glove and practice batting in a backyard or alley. Other times they go to the park to play volleyball, or just to see what is going on. If no one has a flat, they

ride their bikes over; otherwise they walk.

Like his friends, Hector likes to read comic books and collect baseball cards. Sometimes they gather their cards or books, meet on the front stoop, and trade. Although the children talk and joke in English, their parents come from Mexico and Central America, and Spanish is the language spoken in their homes.

When Hector and Polo are drawing or doing their homework at the kitchen table, they often tell stories to each other in English. They speak as fast as they can so their mother will not understand them. Rosario gets annoyed because she suspects they do it just to tease her.

Although Hector and Polo speak English equally well, their parents think it proper that their eldest boy be the family spokesperson. Hector enjoys the responsibility. Whenever someone who can only speak English telephones them, Hector is called to the phone. Or when Rosario has to get a prescription filled at the drugstore, Hector goes along to talk to the pharmacist.

Hector did not speak English when he started kindergarten. It was a scary time. He was away from his mother and brothers. He understood only a few English words and did not know what was going on in class. In first grade Hector had trouble learning to read. But he was determined to learn English, and by the end of the second grade he was reading and writing as well as his classmates. School started to be fun.

Now Hector is a fifth grader, one of the big kids. In United States history, his class is reading about the different immigrant groups who helped settle the West. Their teacher says, "We are a nation of immigrants. Indians, also called Native Americans, have lived here for thousands of years. Everyone else has come to the continental United States from some other place." Then she smiles and says, "Let's find out about us."

The students in Hector's class are told to ask their parents about their ancestors and then write a brief history of their families. It is an exciting project.

When they finish their reports, they will glue snapshots of themselves to their papers and hang them on the wall. But first they get to read them aloud.

Philip traces his family back as far as his great-great-great-grandmother. His ancestors lived on a small Philippine island. Many of them were fishermen. Philip, his sister, and his parents are the only people in his family who have settled in the United States.

One side of Nicky's family came from Norway and Germany. His other ancestors came from Ireland and Sweden. All of them were farmers, and when they came to this country they homesteaded land, which means they farmed and built a house on uncultivated public land that then became theirs under a special homestead law.

Vanessa's great-great-grandmother was a Yaqui Indian from Sonora, Mexico. Her grandfather fought in the

Mexican Revolution. Another one of her ancestors was French.

Erick is descended from Ukrainian, German, and Italian immigrants. His German grandfather and Ukrainian grandmother met in a prisoner-of-war camp. When they were released, they married and came to the United States by ship.

Julie is of French, Irish, and Spanish descent. Her Great-Great-Grandma Elm was born in Texas. When Elm was a child her family moved to California. They traveled by covered wagon.

Everyone is interested in Kyria's family history. One of her African ancestors was a soldier in the American Revolution. Another fought for the Confederacy in the Civil War. Other members of her family homesteaded in Oklahoma.

Hector tells the class about his Mexican ancestors. They were farmers and carpenters.

ANASTASIA

by Shannon Liffland, Grade 3

My great-grandfather and my great-grandmother were Russian Jews who were chased from Russia during the Bolshevic War. They had to travel by foot and pull a large wagon carrying only what they needed to survive. They had to travel at night so that no one would see them because they would be captured by the soldiers. The reason they were leaving their homeland was because the new government did not want any Jewish people living in their country. My great-grandparents got out of Russia alive and eventually came to live in America.

My great-grandfather, Isaac, was a dollmaker who made many beautiful dolls for the very rich children in Russia. Before he left, he gave all of his dolls to the poor children in his village. One of the dolls he didn't give away was Anastasia because it was the most beautiful doll he had ever created. He kept Anastasia to give to his own child some day.

He wrapped Anastasia carefully and placed her in the wagon. Just before my great-grandparents crossed the border safely out of Russia, they met a young couple with a small, beautiful child who was very frightened by the war. Her parents told my great-grandfather that the little girl would no longer speak because she had seen her home burned by the soldiers. Isaac felt so sad that he gave the little girl his best doll, Anastasia. Right after he gave Anastasia to the frightened girl, Isaac heard the soldiers getting closer, so my great-grandparents left Russia forever.

Many years later when my great-grandfather was working in his doll shop in America, a very beautiful woman came in with a small sad child holding a broken doll. The woman handed the doll to Isaac and asked him to fix it. Putting on his glasses, my great-grandfather cried out, "Anastasia!" The woman looked very surprised, and my great-grandfather asked her where she got the doll. The woman told him the story of a very kind man who gave her the doll when she was a child leaving Russia. The woman said her parents told her that she had not spoken for many months until that night when she was given the doll.

Isaac was very happy to see Anastasia again, and even more happy that he had helped the frightened little girl long ago.

THE END

SAIGON

OF VIETNAM

by Linh To Sinh My Bui, age 13

Oh, those wonderful days in Saigon!
Walking bare-footed on the street,
    with other girls who also loved
    to feel the hot sand
    beneath their feet.
So hot
    it felt like the sun
    had dropped fire on our feet.
Looking through the glass windows
    of the stores,
Wondering what to buy
    with the money my mother gave me.
Life was wonderful.

As I grew up in Saigon,
       everything turned out differently.
When I was eight—
             counting in American,
When I was nine—
             counting in Vietnamese,
life became poorer.
Some thought about leaving
       their own country.
And I was one of them.
Young people said goodbye
       to the old ones
       of their family.
And the young ones said
Good luck to the old ones
       on their way to their new life—
       the life they would have
       after they died.

It was dark and cold when the tiny boat
       began to float away from the land of Vietnam.
I didn't want to leave,
but for my future,
I must.
My heart was full of pain when I left.

Oh! My poor country! Whenever can I see you again?
Goodbye Vietnam.
My love country.

My moccasins have not walked

by Duke Redbird

My moccasins have not walked
Among the giant forest trees

My leggings have not brushed
Against the fern and berry bush

My medicine pouch has not been filled
with roots and herbs and sweetgrass

My hands have not fondled the spotted fawn

My eyes have not beheld
The golden rainbow of the north

My hair has not been adorned
With the eagle feather

Yet
My dreams are dreams of these
My heart is one with them
The scent of them caresses my soul

thinking about it

1   Get to know Hector! For thousands of years kids have moved to new places and survived. They've found a place for themselves and had fun. If you were explaining all of this to Hector to help him celebrate himself, how would you do it?

2   Photographs, poems, articles, stories—all of these can tell about a person's roots. If someone wanted to put your roots in a book, what would you tell that person to use?

3   Hector's fifth grade gave class reports. Figure out some other ways a fifth-grade class could present a history of their families. Demonstrate one.

Another Book About New Americans
We Came from Vietnam by Muriel Stanek lets us follow a Vietnamese refugee family as they adjust to a new life in a new land.

Pecos Bill's

Widow-Maker

by Margaret Hodges

You're asking did I ever see Pecos Bill? See him myself? Well, yes and no. I mean, I'm not *that* old. Pecos Bill showed up in the West about the time there began to be cowboys, and that's more than a hundred years ago. You might say he's the granddaddy of all the cowboys you see today. But then again, I've seen *your* granddaddy, knew him well. Every time I look at you, I can see him. And every time I see a cowboy at a rodeo, I'm seeing Pecos Bill, because he taught them everything they know. To tell you the truth, I don't think he's dead yet. If he had been dead, famous as he is, there would have been headlines in all the papers, wouldn't there? So he must be out there still, if you looked for him in the right places. Of course that would mean a fair-sized piece of real estate, from Texas up through Montana on both sides of the Rockies. You could skip the cities and all around the superhighways and head on into the prairies where it's wide and empty, but it would still be some search.

They say Bill's ma and pa were looking for a wide empty place when Bill got born. The family kept moving west every time they'd see smoke going up from a chimney ten miles away. It gave them a smothery feeling to have any folks so close. So they'd put all the children in the old covered wagon and go on again. I don't know just where Bill was born. Maybe in that covered wagon, or maybe in a little old sod hut somewhere in Texas. I heard his ma fed him panther milk and let him cut his teeth on a bowie knife. Anyway, he must have been a knee baby by the time they got to the Pecos River, and he was sound asleep in the very back of the wagon when a rear wheel hit a stone, and he fell out. His pa and ma didn't even know he was missing till she made some flapjacks a couple of weeks later and passed them out, twelve for every child. There was one pile left over, and that's when they noticed Bill was gone.

They went back a good piece, but they never found him, and his ma said, "I'll bet he fell out when we hit that stone at the Pecos River." So that's why they called him Pecos Bill when they talked about him— Pecos for the river, and Bill because it sounded good.

They never would have found him, because he had gone off with an old coyote. I've heard it was the same one that brought fire to the Indians and showed them how to keep warm and to cook. Anyway, that coyote was a real wise one. He took Bill back to his cave and taught him to keep alive on the prairie and find something to eat and water to drink any time of year, no matter how hot or how cold, and to keep going all day without a rest, and to sleep on the ground at night. He taught Bill to howl, too.

So Bill grew up thinking he was a coyote. You'd never believe how big he grew. He had wide shoulders and narrow hips and long legs. The soles of his feet were hard and tough like a coyote's, and his toes had claws, which are a lot more useful than toenails when it comes to living on the prairie. All that time he never wore any clothes or saw a human being, only animals—buffalo, and wild cattle and horses and such. He could talk to any kind of animals in their own language, even mountain lions and snakes, when he got near enough to hear how they talked. Naturally, he was very good at talking to coyotes, and they liked him a lot. When food was scarce, Bill would go off and catch a wild steer by the tail. Then he would kill it with his bare hands and take it home so the coyotes could have a good meal.

How did Bill find out he wasn't a coyote? Well, about the time he was grown, there started to be cowboys out West, and Bill would make himself invisible and listen to them talking at night around a campfire. He got so he could talk the same way they did, only better. Then one day when he got good and ready, he came right up to a cowboy who was on his horse, watering a few cattle at a river. The cowboy was scared half to death when he saw how big Bill was.

"Who are you?" he asked, with his teeth chattering.

"I'm a coyote," said Pecos Bill.

"No, you're not," said the cowboy. "You're a man. Where are your clothes?"

"Coyotes don't wear clothes," Pecos Bill told him.

"Here are two blankets," the cowboy said. "Make yourself some pants."

So Bill decided to look at himself in the river and find out whether he was a coyote or a man. When he found out he was a man, he thought he'd throw in with humans, so he took the two blankets and made himself a shirt. Then he laid hold of an old steer's tail and yelled "Yee-ow!" like a wild coyote, and that steer was so scared he jumped right out of his skin. Pecos Bill took the hide and made himself some cowboy chaps. They were the first ones, and Bill invented them. He wouldn't have done it if it had been winter, because it took the steer six weeks to grow a new hide. Bill was kind—tough but kind.

How did he find out he was the Pecos Bill that had fallen out of the wagon? To tell the truth, I don't know, and I aim to tell nothing but the truth. Just keep still and listen.

So he said good-bye to the coyotes and went off with Smitty—that was the name of the cowboy—to the ranch where he worked, and Smitty helped him get some clothes that fitted, and a hat. The other cowboys all wore ten-gallon hats, but Pecos Bill had to wear a forty-gallon hat. He got some boots, too. Cowboys wore tight boots to make their feet look small, and Bill hated those boots.

Whenever he could, he'd take them off and go barefoot. That way he could run faster than any horse.

Of course, Pecos Bill had learned to ride a bronco
the very first day at the ranch, but he never needed to
own one. He just rode to show the cowboys how to
rope a steer from the saddle and then jump off and
hogtie it. They never could do that before Bill came.
And no one could break a bronco the way he could.
He'd take off his boots and jump on the back of the
wild animal. Then he'd get a grip on the mane and
dig in with the claws on his toes. That bronco could
try bucking and cakewalking—that's when he
tilts backward on his hind legs—and corkscrewing
and high diving, but Bill would hang on until the
horse quieted down and gave up so he could be
saddled and bridled.

One thing Bill found out right away at the ranch
was that the cowboys didn't do much work. They'd
take the cattle to water or pasture, but the rest of the
time they mostly sat around the ranch chewing

tobacco and telling lies about how great they were. They were supposed to catch wild cattle and bring them back to the herd, but the best they could do was to spread a noose on the prairie and hope an animal would walk into it. Cattle were always wandering off, too, and getting lost, so the herds stayed pretty puny. But Pecos Bill changed all that. He knew the prairies were full of wild cattle just waiting to be caught. So he thought about it for a while, and then he came up with a new invention. He got a couple of old steer hides the same way I told you, and he made them into one long, thin strip with a noose at the end. It was the first lariat, and Bill started practicing how to throw it, until he could rope in anything he aimed at. After a while, all cowboys had lariats. None of them could bring down an animal as fast as Bill could, but pretty soon the herds began to grow. Then Bill had a better idea. He made a lariat long

enough to go around the world, and when he saw a big herd of cattle, he'd rope the whole lot of them with one throw and bring them on back to the ranch.

A big problem in those days was telling whose cattle were whose. Herds would get mixed up on the range, and cowboys from different ranches would start shooting each other for stealing. Well, Pecos Bill showed the ranch blacksmith how to make a branding iron, and it wasn't long before all the ranchers were branding their cattle. It wasn't much fun for the cattle, but you can see it was better in the long run.

Then Pecos Bill said to the men, "This is a whole new kind of cowpunching. Starting now, we're going to ride all day long to keep the herd together, and we've got to take turns riding the herd all night too. When we aren't riding at night, we'll sleep on the ground. We won't be eating at the ranch much, either. We'll eat from a chuck wagon that will go right along with us on the range. In the spring we'll have a big roundup, and then we'll ride herd along the trail to market. And we're really going to look after the dogies." What are dogies? They're poor little motherless calves.

Well, at first the men said this sounded too much like work. But Pecos Bill said, "You've been telling lies all along about how great you were. Now you're going to *be* great." Then he went off all over the West to show cowboys how to work, and they have been great ever since.

As I said, Bill never had wanted a horse of his own because he could outrun any horse he had ever seen. But to make traveling easy he tamed a mountain lion and put a saddle and bridle on it. You should have seen them, Bill whooping and yelling and waving his hat, and the mountain lion going a hundred feet at every jump. Bill tamed a rattlesnake, too, and looped it over his saddle horn. When he made it whip around, it was the best quirt a cowboy ever had.

It must have been when Bill was off on his travels that he heard about a great pacing white stallion. A pacer puts his two left feet forward at the same time and then his two right feet, which is the easiest and smoothest way a horse can go. Bill heard that this white stallion was the biggest and fastest and most beautiful horse in the world, with a whole herd of pretty mares following after him. Some cowboys said they didn't believe there was any such animal, because if there was, it would have to have been sired by the

flying horse with wings in the story thousands of years ago. But finally Bill met some cowboys who claimed they had seen the horse, so Bill made up his mind to find him. The men said they had tried to catch him the best way it could be done. Each man had a string of horses and covered all the trails for miles around every time they'd catch sight of the stallion. But they couldn't any more than just keep him in sight, even though they changed to fresh horses all the time and ran those horses till they dropped. They went on chasing him for a week, and the stallion never even changed his pace.

When Pecos Bill heard this, he wanted to see the

white horse more than he had ever wanted anything, but it took him about two years of traveling, from the Southwest clear out to the Pacific Coast and way up into Canada.

Then one night he camped in the Crazy Mountains. You think I'm joking? Look them up on the map. They're there, in Montana. Anyway, in the morning Bill thought he saw the sun coming up with a white cloud on each side of it. When he looked again, he saw it was a horse, not white like they had told him, but a palomino, pale

gold with a white mane and a white tail, and Pecos Bill knew this was the horse he had been looking for. He gave a neigh you could hear to Kingdom Come, and he heard an answer. He didn't know if it was his own voice echoing in the mountains or the neigh of the palomino, far off, like a bugle call. Then he saw the horse was coming toward him, and he made himself invisible for a while, but neighing all the time, until the stallion came up right beside him, head and tail up, looking proud and free.

Bill made himself visible again and started to talk in horse language as nice as could be. But the palomino was suspicious. He shied and snorted, and Bill saw he was going to run, so he threw his lariat right over that sleek neck. Then he pulled back and dug in his heels, but the stallion reared up and came down with his front hoofs so hard and sharp that the leather snapped in two. He shook off the noose and went like a streak of greased lightning with Bill after him. They covered the West from Montana to Mexico and back again before Bill got the palomino cornered in a gulch and did a flipflop onto his back, landing face forward. That's quite a trick, and you can still see cowboys do it in a rodeo. Bill taught them.

Anyway, before he could get hold with his hands or toes, the stallion arched his back so high and fast that Bill went several miles into the air. He came down wedged between some jagged rocks like a pickle in the top of a pickle bottle. This saved his life, because those rocks were so sharp they could have speared him like a pickle fork. But he pulled himself together and saw the palomino right below him, standing still, waiting to find out if Bill was gone for good. Bill dropped straight down on the stallion's back, and this time he got a good grip with both hands in the thick mane. He dug his claws into the ribs and hung on tight with his knees.

Well, the stallion tried every way in the world to throw Bill off. He corkscrewed and cakewalked and reared high up—that's what they call "skyscraping"—and jumped a mile back and two miles forward, but Bill hung on. The stallion had one more trick, crashing down to earth on his back to crush his rider under him. But Bill had a trick to match that one. He slid out before the horse landed. Then he sat down on the neck, putting his heel on the cheek. The harder the palomino struggled, the harder Bill came down on the cheek, and at the same time he started to sweet-talk the horse, patting him on the shoulder and stroking his nose. Bill said that he was the greatest cowboy of all time and he wanted the greatest horse that ever lived to be his partner and help him make the American West the greatest cattle country in the world.

The palomino started to listen. Bill promised he would never try to break his spirit, because he was wild and free himself and he wouldn't want his horse to be any other way. Then, to show he was telling the truth, he got up and walked off a way, leaving the horse to decide what he wanted to do. The palomino leaped to his feet and stood for a few minutes, trying to make up his mind. Then he went and nuzzled Bill's shoulder.

When Bill came back to the ranch riding the palomino, the eyes of the other cowboys popped out. They couldn't believe what they were seeing, especially when Bill jumped down and the horse stayed by his shoulder.

Smitty said, "I want to ride that horse just once, Bill."

"Better not," Bill said.

But Smitty wouldn't take no for an answer. He made a run and landed on the palomino's back. Well, he didn't stay there long. A second later he was up in the air and out of sight. The other cowboys had to ask around for quite a spell to find out if he had landed somewhere, and finally they heard he was up on top of Pikes Peak and couldn't get down. So Pecos Bill shook out his lariat and threw. He caught Smitty around the middle and tightened the noose. Then he pulled him in. You should have seen Smitty. Every bone in his body was broken. The cowboys couldn't help feeling sorry for him, even though it was his own fault, so Bill laid him out straight in his bunk with all his bones back in place, and in about two weeks he was in perfect shape again. He thanked Pecos Bill for saving his life and asked, "Bill, has that horse got a name?"

"Not that I know of," Bill answered.

"Well, then," said Smitty, "call him Widow-Maker."

So that's how Bill's famous horse got his name.

From then on, nothing could stop the American West from being the greatest cattle country in the world, because Pecos Bill and Widow-Maker were in charge of everything.

You'd think Bill would have been perfectly happy now that he had Widow-Maker, but sometimes he got pretty lonely out on the prairie, just the way the other cowboys did, so he taught them songs to quiet the cattle or sing around the campfire at night. Pecos Bill wrote all the cowboy songs. One of them was:

> *"I'm a poor lonesome cowboy,*
> *I'm a poor lonesome cowboy,*
> *I'm a poor lonesome cowboy,*
> *And a long way from home."*

It was easy to learn and all the cowboys sang it. It sounded nice and sad, sort of like a bunch of coyotes howling, especially when one cowboy would play the tune on a mouth organ. The song went on:

> *"I ain't got no father,*
> *I ain't got no mother,*
> *No sister and no brother*
> *To ride along with me.*

> *"I ain't got no sweetheart,*
> *I ain't got no sweetheart,*
> *I ain't got no sweetheart*
> *To sit and talk with me."*

Pecos Bill got to wishing he had a sweetheart, but there were no ladies on the range, and the girls in the cowtowns were no ladies, either. Anyway, not too many cowboys got married. They didn't want to be hogtied by a woman. But one day when Bill was down on the Rio Grande, he saw a pretty girl riding a catfish, with just a girth cinched around it for her to hold on by. And those catfish in the Rio Grande are bigger than whales. That got Bill interested, so he asked around and found out that she lived on a dude ranch where tenderfoots, people from the East, could come and pretend to be cowboys for a summer. The girl's name was Slue-foot Sue and she helped her ma and her pa run the ranch. They called her Slue-foot because she could dance and kick up her heels and twirl around better than any other girl when they started square dancing at a hoedown. She had her own horse, too, and when she was riding in her buckskin shirt and chaps and wearing a sombrero, she was the best-looking cowboy that ever wore spurs, except of course she was a cowgirl.

Bill was almost too bashful to speak to her, but she helped him out. She kept looking at him and singing to him:

"As I was a-walkin' one morning for pleasure
I spied a cowpuncher a-ridin' along;
His hat was throwed back and his spurs was
*   a-jinglin',*
And as he approached he was singin' this song—
'Whoopee ti yi yo, git along, little dogies,
It's your misfortune and none of my own,
Whoopee ti yi yo, git along, little dogies,
For you know Wyoming will be your new home.'"

From this Bill got the idea that Slue-foot Sue liked him, too, and since she liked everything else he liked, he finally got up his nerve to ask her to marry him. She said yes right away.

Well, everything went along fine till the wedding. That day Sue wore a white silk dress with a steel-spring bustle that was all the style, and she looked as pretty as a picture. After the wedding she said, "Oh, Bill, you said you loved me. Will you promise me one thing?"

"Why, sure," Bill said. "Anything you want, Sue." He was plain loco about her.

"Whoopee!" said Sue. "Let me ride Widow-Maker!"

"You can't do that!" Bill told her, and he explained what had happened when Smitty tried to ride the stallion.

"You promised!" Sue yelled. And with that she jumped on the back of the palomino. Well, the next minute she was up in the sky, and when she came down again, she landed on the steel-spring bustle and bounced up again as high as the moon. In fact, she had to dodge to keep from hitting it. What was worse, she kept on bouncing up and down for about a week, until Bill finally got where she was coming down and caught her. After that, Slue-foot Sue didn't ask to ride Widow-Maker any more, and she and Bill got along fine.

What do I think happened to them? Well, it stands to reason that Pecos Bill would have found a good place to live, smart as he was and knowing every inch of every state all over the West. So I think he must have found a nice valley that nobody else knew about, where it never snowed and never got too hot either, and where there was plenty of water and green grass for Widow-Maker and his herd of mares. And Bill and Sue would have had enough children to help them run the best ranch in the West. Of course, after a while, they weren't so young anymore, but they didn't get old either, not so you could notice it. Widow-Maker? Well, he surely sired some beautiful colts and fillies, didn't he? Because if you go out West you can still see palominos with pale-gold coats and white manes and tails, and it's just like seeing the granddaddy of them all, Pecos Bill's Widow-Maker.

thinking about it

1 Of course this is a tall tale. You can't quite believe it. Yet you go on reading because it has something new and surprising at every twist and turn, like watching  Widow-Maker at his feistiest. Which twists and turns did you find newest and most surprising?

2 Credibility—that's what the tall tale teller is really after. Credibility means making the story believable, even when the listener knows that it doesn't tell quite what happened. How does the author of this tall tale help make the tale credible?

3 Just one more adventure. Think of one more thing that Pecos Bill could have invented. What is it and how did he invent it? Is your addition to Pecos Bill's lore new, surprising, and credible? Make it so.

More American Tall Tales
If you enjoy tall tales, you might have fun reading *Whoppers, Tall Tales, and Other Lies: Collected from American Folklore* by Alvin Schwartz.

Speaking of Uncle Remus

by JULIUS LESTER

The hero of this story is named Brer Rabbit. (Brer was the way slaves said the word, *Brother.*) Brer Rabbit seems to have one purpose in life— to get in trouble. Well, that's not quite true because there is one thing he does even better. He gets *out* of trouble.

Brer Rabbit might be little in the body but he is large in the brain. That's where it counts!

Brer Rabbit is also mighty of mouth. Brer Rabbit has enough mouth for a roomful of ears. When his brain and mouth start working at the same time and at the same speed, you better be careful. That rabbit can trick the white off rice.

Don't you wish you were smart enough to think and talk yourself out of trouble? I wish I were!

So, you're about to read a story about Brer Rabbit. But, you can't have a story without a storyteller. That would be like trying to have rain without any wet.

You see my name and my picture. That doesn't mean I'm the one telling the story. I am, but then again, I'm not.

If I came to your school and you asked me to talk about Brer Rabbit, I couldn't do that and still be me. Before you could blink your eye, I would stop being me and become an old man named Uncle Remus. He even talks different than I do—

"Don't nobody rightly know where Brer Rabbit come from. Some say he from Africa. I know better than that. He's got plenty of kin people in Africa— aunts and uncles and cousins, in-laws, outlaws, and no-laws. But he was born right here in these United States.

"Now don't come asking me when his birthday is. Folks didn't have calendars with numbers on 'em back in them days.

"And don't come asking me where he was born. I know he was born in the briar patch, but whether it was a briar patch in Georgia or Texas or on MTV, I don't remember. What's important is that he was born.

"Now, what do you think was the first thing Brer Rabbit thought about when he was born?

"No, it was not chocolate. But you're on the right track. The first thing he thought about was eating. And what you think he wanted to eat?

"If you said vegetables, you said a mouthful. And that reminds me. Seems to me there's a story wandering around somewhere on the backside of my brain about the time Brer Rabbit just couldn't stay away from Mr. Man's garden. . . ."

Brer Rabbit Goes Back to Mr. Man's Garden

as told by JULIUS LESTER
illustrated by JERRY PINKNEY

Mr. Man's garden was too delicious-looking for Brer Rabbit to leave alone. And anyway, it wasn't right for Mr. Man to have all them pretty vegetables to himself. Obviously, he didn't believe in sharing. Being worried about Mr. Man's soul, Brer Rabbit decided he'd *make* Mr. Man share.

A few mornings later Mr. Man went to town. As he was leaving he hollered to his daughter, "Janey! Don't

you let Brer Rabbit get in my green peas. You hear me?"

"Yes, Daddy," she said.

Brer Rabbit was hiding in the bushes, listening. Soon as Mr. Man left, Brer Rabbit walked up to the little girl as bold as day.

"Ain't you Janey?" he asked.

"My daddy call me Janey. What your daddy call you?"

"Well, my daddy dead, but when he was living he called me Billy Malone." He smiled. "I passed your daddy in the road and he said for me to come tell you to give me some sparrow grass."

Janey had been warned against Brer Rabbit, but not

Billy Malone, so she opened the gate and let Brer Rabbit into the garden. Brer Rabbit got as much sparrow grass as he could carry and left.

Mr. Man came back and saw that somebody had been in his garden. He asked Janey about it. She told him that Billy Malone said it was all right for him to go in and get some sparrow grass. Mr. Man knew something was up but didn't say anything.

Next morning when he got ready to go, he told Janey to keep an eye out for Brer Rabbit and not let *anybody* get any sparrow grass.

When Mr. Man was out of sight, Brer Rabbit come walking down the road and greeted the little girl, bowing low like a real gentleman. "I saw your daddy just now. He said I couldn't have no sparrow grass today, but it would be all right if I helped myself to the English peas."

The little girl opened the gate and Brer Rabbit made off with enough English peas to feed all of England.

When Mr. Man came back, his pea vines looked like a storm had hit 'em, and he was hot! "Who been in my peas?" he asked his daughter.

"Mr. Billy Malone," she said.

"What this Billy Malone look like?"

"He got a split lip, pop eyes, big ears, and a bobtail, Daddy."

Mr. Man didn't have a bit of trouble recognizing that description. He fixed a box trap and set it in the garden among the peanuts. The next morning he told

Janey, "Now, whatever you do today, don't let nobody have any sparrow grass, and don't let 'em get any more English peas, the few I got left."

Soon as Mr. Man was out of sight, here come Brer Rabbit. He bowed low and said, "Good morning, Miz Janey. I met your daddy down the road there and he said I can't have no more sparrow grass or English peas, but to help myself to the peanuts."

Janey let him in the garden. Brer Rabbit headed straight for the peanut patch, where he tripped the string and the box fell right on top of him. He was caught and he knew it.

Wasn't long before Mr. Man came back. He went to the peanut patch and saw the overturned box. He stooped down, peered through the slats, and saw Brer Rabbit inside, quivering.

Mr. Man whooped. "Yes, sir! I got you this time, you devil! I got you! And when I get through with you, ain' gon' be nothing left. I'm gon' carry your foot in my pocket, put your meat in the pot, and wear your fur on my head."

Words like that always put a chill up and down Brer Rabbit's spine. "Mr. Man, I know I done wrong. And if you let me go, I promise I'll stay away from your garden."

Mr. Man chuckled. "You gon' stay away from my garden if I don't let you go too. I got to go to the house to get my butcher knife."

Mr. Man went to the house, but he forgot to close the garden gate behind him. Brer Fox came down the road, and seeing the open gate, took it as an invitation and walked on in. He heard something hollering and making a lot of racket. He wandered around until he found the noise coming from underneath a box. "What the dickens is that?" he asked.

Brer Rabbit would've known that voice anywhere. "Run, Brer Fox! Run! Get out of here right now if you care about your life!"

"What's wrong, Brer Rabbit?"

"Mr. Man trapped me in here and is making me eat lamb. I'm about to bust wide open I done ate so much lamb. Run, Brer Fox, before he catch you."

Brer Fox wasn't thinking about running. "How's the lamb?"

"It tastes good at first, but enough is enough and too much is plenty. You better get out of here before he catches you."

Brer Fox wasn't running anywhere. "I like lamb, Brer Rabbit." He took the box off Brer Rabbit. "Put the box over me." Brer Rabbit did so gladly and decided not to wait around for the next chapter.

The story don't say what happened to Brer Fox. Brer Rabbit took care of himself. Now it's up to Brer Fox to take care of himself. That's the name of that tune.

thinking about it

1 You are Mr. Man. Should you just give up and invite Brer Rabbit in for a salad? You are Brer Rabbit. Would you accept an invitation? Give your reasons.

2 Uncle Remus is the storyteller of "Brer Rabbit Goes Back to Mr. Man's Garden." How would the story have been different if someone else, say Janey or Mr. Man, had told it?

3 What's next? Will Brer Rabbit come back? What will happen to Brer Fox? What will we find out when we tune in tomorrow for the next episode?

Another Book About Uncle Remus and Brer Rabbit
You could spend a whole day curled up with the Brer Rabbit stories. Try this one for starters: *More Tales of Uncle Remus* by Julius Lester.

Her Seven Brothers

Story and illustrations by **Paul Goble**

Do you know what the birds and animals say?

In the old days there were more people who understood them.

The Creator did not intend them to speak in our way; theirs is the language of the spirits. Yes, birds and animals, butterflies and beetles, stones and trees still speak to us; but we have to learn how to listen.

In those distant times there was a girl who lived with her parents. She did not have any brothers or sisters, but she was never alone because she could speak with the birds and animals. She understood the spirits of all things.

When the girl was quite young her mother taught her how to embroider with dyed porcupine quills onto deer and buffalo skin robes and clothes. She worked hard. In time she became very good at it. Her parents were proud when she gave away something she had made. People marveled at her skill and beautiful designs. They believed that Porcupine, who climbs trees closest to Sun himself, had spoken to the girl and given her mysterious help to do such wonderful work. While the girl worked, she kept good thoughts in her mind; she knew that she could not make anything beautiful without help from the spirits.

One day she started to sew clothes for a man: a shirt and a pair of moccasins. She decorated them with porcupine quills in brightly colored patterns. Every design had a meaning for her.

When the shirt and moccasins were finished, she did not give them to anyone; she put them away and

started on another set. Her parents wondered why
she did this when she had neither brothers nor young
men who were courting her. When a second set was
finished and she was starting another, her mother
asked her for whom she was making the clothes.

Her daughter replied: "There are seven brothers
who live by themselves far in the north country
where the cold wind comes from. I have seen them in
my mind when I close my eyes. I am making the

clothes for them. They have no sister. I will look for the trail that leads to their tipi. I will ask them to be my brothers."

At first her mother thought it was just a young girl's imagining, but every day her daughter brought out her work. The months passed, and she made six shirts and pairs of moccasins. And then she started with special care on a seventh set, smaller than the others, to fit a very small boy. Her mother was puzzled, and yet she sensed that her daughter had seen something wonderful. Even the wise men did not know, but they believed that the unseen powers had spoken to the girl.

Her mother said: "I will go with you. When the snow melts we will pack your gifts onto the dogs. I will help you guide them until you find the trail."

The geese brought back the springtime, and they set out for the north country. The way was green and beautiful with flowers; and loud with frogs and red-winged blackbirds calling by every pond. Two faithful dogs carried the bags of clothes. The girl had the little boy's clothes in a separate bundle on her back.

When the girl found the trail, she said to her mother: "This is where I will go on alone. Mother, do not be sad! You will be proud! Soon you will see me again with my brothers; everyone will know and love us!"

But her mother did cry. She called to the sun: "O Sun, look after my child!" She watched her daughter, leading a dog at either hand, walk away and fade slowly into the immensity of the blue distance.

The girl walked on for many days into the land of pine trees until she came at last to a tipi pitched close to a lake. It was painted yellow and had stars all over it. The door was partly open; she thought she could see bright eyes peering at her from inside.

She unpacked the bags from the dogs. After they had taken a drink at the lake, she thanked them. "Now go straight back home," she told them. "Keep to the trail, and do not chase rabbits."

A little boy ran out of the tipi and called to her: "I am glad you have come! I have been waiting for you! You have come looking for brothers. I have six older brothers. They are away hunting buffalo, but they will be back this evening. They will be surprised to see you; they do not have my power of knowing and seeing. I am glad to call you 'Sister.'"

The girl opened the bundle of clothes she had made for him. "Younger Brother," she said, "this is my gift to you."

The boy had never seen anything so beautiful; his clothes had always been plain, and often old. He put on his new shirt and moccasins and scampered down to the lake to take a look at himself in the water. The girl untied the other bags, and placed a shirt and pair of moccasins on each of the six beds around the tipi.

When the little boy heard his brothers returning, he ran out of the tipi to meet them. "Wherever did you get those fine clothes?" they asked.

The boy replied: "A girl made them for me. She came looking for brothers, and now I call her 'Sister.'

She has made wonderful shirts for all of you.
Come and see!"

The brothers were very proud of their sister
and looked after her well. While they were out
hunting, she stayed in the tipi with the little
boy. He would take his bow and arrows to
protect her if she went out for water or to gather
firewood. She liked to have good meals ready for the
hunters when they returned home.

They all lived happily together until a day when a
little buffalo calf came to the tipi. He scratched at the
door with his hoof. The boy went outside and asked:

"What do you want, Buffalo Calf?"

"I have been sent by the chief of the
Buffalo Nation," the calf said. "He wants your sister.
Tell her to follow me."

"He cannot have her," the boy answered. "My
sister is happy here. We are proud of her."

The calf ran away, but in a little while a yearling
bull galloped up to the tipi and bellowed: "I have
been sent by the chief of the Buffalo Nation. He
insists on having your sister. Tell her to come."

"No! He will never have her," the boy answered. "Go away!"

It was not long before an old bull with sharp curved horns charged up and thundered: "The chief of the Buffalo Nation demands your sister *now!* She must come *at once,* or he will come with the whole Buffalo Nation and get her, and you will all be killed." He shook his mane and whipped his back with his tail in rage.

"No!" the boy shouted. "He will never have her. Look! There are my big brothers coming back. *Hurry,* or they will surely kill you!"

When the brothers heard what had happened they were afraid. Even then they sensed an uncertain rumble, like shaking deep down inside the earth. Beyond the horizon dark dust clouds were rolling out across the sky toward them. The Buffalo People were stampeding in the awful darkness beneath.

"Run!" shouted one of the brothers.

"Wait!" the little boy called out, and he ran into the tipi for his bow and arrows. He shot an arrow straight up into the air and a pine tree appeared, growing upward with the arrow's flight.

The girl quickly lifted her little brother onto the lowest branch and climbed up after him. All the brothers clambered after, just as the Chief of the Buffalo struck the tree a terrible blow, splintering it with his horns. He hooked at the trunk again and again and it was split into slivers. Dark masses of angry buffalo crowded around the tree, pawing the ground and bellowing. The tree quivered and started to topple.

"Hurry! You have power. Save us!" the brothers called to the little boy. He shot an arrow and the tree grew taller.

He shot another far into the sky and the tree grew straight upward, higher and higher, and they were carried far away up among the stars.

And there they all jumped down from the branches onto the boundless star-prairies of the world above.

The girl and her seven brothers are still there. They are the Seven Stars in the northern sky, which we call the Big Dipper. But look carefully and you will see that there are really eight stars in the Big Dipper; close to one of them there is a tiny star; it is the little boy walking with his sister. She is never lonely now. They are forever turning around the Star Which Always Stands Still, the North Star. It is good to know that they once lived here on earth.

Listen to the stars! We are never alone at night.

pulling it all together

1 Close your eyes and picture *Her Seven Brothers* as a dance. What movements would you use to tell each event?

2 In this book you've read about a variety of Americans. The book is like an enormous room where these Americans wait for you to find out about them. What will you say to them, and what will you learn?

3 A quilt, a mural, a hanging mobile — what object could show people this variety of Americans?

Frederic Remington
*by Ernest Raboff
and Adeline Peter*
Harper, 1988
See the American Old West through the eyes of this famous cowboy artist.

A Lion To Guard Us
by Clyde Robert Bulla
Harper, 1981
It is the year 1609. You are sailing from England to the colony of Virginia in North America with three children who are searching for their father. What adventures await you?

The Bells of Christmas
by Virginia Hamilton
Harcourt Brace Jovanovich, 1990
What was Christmas like in 1890? Take a journey back in time to experience the joys of a young boy's Christmas.

Nancy Hanks of Wilderness Road
by Meridel LeSueur
Knopf, 1990
Nancy Hanks, Abe Lincoln's mother, dreamed that Abe would get an education and make something of himself. Here is the story of her struggles to help her son.

The Story of Jumping Mouse
by John Steptoe
Lothrop, Lee &
Shepard, 1984
In this traditional Native American legend, a spunky little mouse makes an almost impossible journey with the help of an unlikely character, Magic Frog.

Making a New Home in America
by Maxine Rosenberg
Lothrop, Lee &
Shepard, 1986
It takes a lot to adjust to a new home in a new land. These four young people tell all about it.

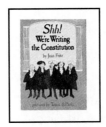

Shh! We're Writing the Constitution
by Jean Fritz
Putnam, 1987
You are there at the writing of the Constitution to experience the heated debates, Ben Franklin's catnaps, and the invasion of the huge bluebottle flies.

Have a Happy . . .
by Mildred Pitts Walter
Lothrop, Lee &
Shepard, 1989
Eleven-year-old Chris has always had to share his birthday with a holiday. This year he's not going to take it lying down!

Biography

A **biography** is the story of a real person's life, written by someone else. It includes information about what the person actually said or did. "The Mysterious Mr. Lincoln" is a biography that includes quotations from Abraham Lincoln. These reveal a lot about Lincoln's thoughts and actions and make reading about him more interesting.

Historical Fiction

Historical fiction is realistic fiction that takes place in the past. The setting is very important to understanding the story. These stories may include real historical figures as well as characters created by the author. "An Errand to Town" and *Samuel's Choice* are historical fiction.

Myth

Myths are often stories that explain something about nature that people had a hard time explaining, like why there are waves in the ocean. *Her Seven Brothers* is a myth that tells how the Big Dipper was formed.

Plot

A **plot** develops when there is conflict between characters, between a character and nature, or within a character. In "Brer Rabbit Goes Back to Mr. Man's Garden," the conflict is between the two main characters. "An Errand to Town" has conflict between characters (Laura and Carrie) and nature (the tall prairie grass that hides Pa). In *Samuel's Choice*, Samuel has conflict within himself when deciding whether or not to help the Patriot soldiers.

Point of View

Point of view is the perspective from which the story is told. Sometimes a story will be told in the first person point of view. In *Samuel's Choice*, Samuel uses words like *I* and *my* when he tells the story. Sometimes a story will be told in the third person, using words like *he, she, they.* An example is "An Errand to Town."

Setting

The **setting** is the time and place in which a story happens. In historical fiction, the setting is very important. The author must describe the way people dress and what their homes are like so that you feel you are in a time and place long ago. In "An Errand to Town," Laura Ingalls Wilder describes Pa using horses to mow, and teams and wagons tied to hitching posts on the town's main street. In *Samuel's Choice*, the soldiers and slaves are described and shown in the clothing of the time. This helps create the setting.

Tall Tales

Tall tales are always full of exaggeration: characters constantly say and do things that are completely unbelievable. The author of "Pecos Bill's Widow-Maker" lets you know Pecos is unusual right from the start. Early in life he was fed panther milk, cut his teeth on a bowie knife, and was raised by a coyote. Everything that he did from then on was downright amazing.

Vocabulary from your selections

ad ven tur ous (ad ven/chər əs), **1** fond of adventures; ready to take risks; daring: *a bold, adventurous explorer.* **2** full of risk; dangerous: *An expedition to the North Pole is an adventurous undertaking. adj.* —**ad ven/tur ous ly,** *adv.* —**ad ven/tur ous ness,** *n.*

ag o nize (ag/ə nīz), **1** feel great anguish; suffer agony. **2** strive painfully; struggle. **3** cause to suffer extreme pain; torture. *v.* **ag o nized, ag o niz ing.** —**ag/o niz/ing ly,** *adv.*

ag o ny (ag/ə nē), very painful suffering; very great anguish: *the agony of a severe toothache. The loss of their child filled them with agony. n., pl.* **ag o nies.**

am bi tion (am bish/ən), **1** a strong desire for fame, honor, wealth, etc.; seeking after a high position or great power: *Because he was filled with ambition, he worked after school and on Saturdays.* **2** thing strongly desired or sought after: *Her ambition is to be an oceanographer. n.* —**am bi/tion less,** *adj.*

am bi tious (am bish/əs), **1** having or guided by ambition; desiring strongly: *She is ambitious to get through high school in three years.* **2** showing or arising from ambition: *an ambitious plan. adj.* —**am bi/tious ly,** *adv.* —**am bi/tious ness,** *n.*

ar chives (är/kīvz), **1** place where public records or historical documents are kept. **2** the public records or historical documents kept in such a place. *n., pl.*

be hold (bi hōld/), look at; see; observe: *to behold a beautiful sunset (v.). Behold! the king! (interj.). v.,* **be held, be hold ing;** *interj.*

brand (brand), **1** a certain kind, grade, or make: *Do you like this brand of flour?* **2** a name or mark that a company uses to distinguish its goods from the goods of others; trademark. **3** an iron stamp for burning a mark. **4** a mark made by burning the skin with a hot iron: *The cattle on this big ranch are identified by a brand which shows who owns them.* **5** to mark by burning the skin with a hot iron. *In former times criminals were often branded.* **6** a mark of disgrace: *He could never rid himself of the brand of coward.* **7** put a mark of disgrace on: *She has been branded as a traitor.* **8** piece of wood that is burning or partly burned. 1-4,6,8 *n.,* 5,7 *v.* —**brand/er,** *n.*

ca ress (kə res/), **1** a touch showing affection; tender embrace or kiss. **2** touch or stroke tenderly; embrace or kiss. 1 *n., pl.* **ca ress es;** 2 *v.* —**ca ress/a ble,** *adj.* —**ca ress/er,** *n.* —**ca ress/ing ly,** *adv.*

chaps (shaps *or* chaps), strong leather trousers without a back, worn over other trousers by cowhands. *n., pl.*

cowboys wearing **chaps**

a	hat	i	it	oi	oil	ch	child	ə	stands for:
ā	age	ī	ice	ou	out	ng	long		a in about
ä	far	o	hot	u	cup	sh	she		e in taken
e	let	ō	open	ù	put	th	thin		i in pencil
ē	equal	ô	order	ü	rule	ŦH	then		o in lemon
ėr	term					zh	measure		u in circus

choice (chois), **1** act of choosing: *She was careful in her choice of friends.* **2** power or chance to choose: *I have my choice between a radio and a camera for my birthday.* **3** person or thing chosen: *This camera is my choice.* **4** thing among several things to be chosen; alternative: *Their action left no choice but to adjourn the meeting.* **5** quantity and variety to choose from: *We found a wide choice of vegetables in the market.* **6** of fine quality; excellent; superior: *The choicest fruit had the highest price.* 1-5 *n.,* 6 *adj.,* **choic er, choic est.** —**choice′less,** *adj.* —**choice′ly,** *adv.* —**choice′ness,** *n.*

con fi dent (kon′fə dənt), having confidence; firmly believing; certain; sure: *I feel confident that our team will win. adj.* —**con′fi dent ly,** *adv.*

cur rent (kėr′ənt), **1** a flow of water, air, or any liquid; running stream: *The current swept the stick down the river. The draft created a current of cold air over my feet.* **2** flow of electricity through a wire, etc.: *The current went off when lightning hit the power lines.* **3** rate or amount of such a flow, usually expressed in amperes: *Heating requires much more current than lighting does.* **4** course or movement (of events or of opinions): *Newspapers influence the current of public opinion.* **5** of the present time. *The current issue of a magazine is the latest one published. We discuss current events in social studies class.* **6** generally used or accepted: *Long ago the belief was current that the earth was flat.* **7** going around; passing from person to person: *A rumor is current that school will close a week early this year.* 1-4 *n.,* 5-7 *adj.* —**cur′rent ness,** *n.*

current (definition 1)

de mand (di mand'), **1** ask for as a right: *demand a trial by jury.* **2** ask for with authority: *The teacher demanded the name of the student who rang the fire alarm.* **3** call for; require; need: *Training a puppy demands patience.* **4** act of demanding: *a demand for a bigger allowance.* **5** thing demanded; claim: *Parents have many demands upon their time.* **6** desire and ability to buy: *Because of the large crop, the supply of apples is greater than the demand.* 1-3 *v.,* 4-6 *n.*
—**de mand'a ble,** *adj.* —**de mand' er,** *n.* **in demand,** wanted: *Taxicabs are much in demand on rainy days.*

de scrip tion (di skrip'shən), **1** a telling in words how a person, place, thing, or an event looks or behaves; describing. **2** composition or account that describes or gives a picture in words: *The reporter's vivid description of the hotel fire made me feel as if I were right at the scene.* **3** kind; sort: *I have seen no dog of any description today. n.*

el o quence (el'ə kwəns), **1** flow of speech that has grace and force: *The jury was moved by the eloquence of the lawyer's words.* **2** power to win by speaking; art of speaking so as to stir the feelings. *n.*

el o quent (el'ə kwənt), **1** having the power of expressing one's feelings or thoughts with grace and force; having eloquence: *an eloquent speaker.* **2** very expressive: *eloquent eyes. adj.* —**el'o quent ly,** *adv.*

em broi der (em broi'dər), **1** ornament (cloth, leather, etc.) with a raised design or pattern of stitches: *embroider a shirt with a colorful design.* **2** make (an ornamental design or pattern) on cloth, leather etc., with stitches: *I embroidered silver stars on my blue jeans.* **3** add imaginary details to; exaggerate: *She often embroiders her stories to make them more interesting. v.* —**em broi'der er,** *n.*

embroidery

etch (ech), **1** engrave (a drawing or design) on a metal plate, glass, etc., by means of acid that eats away the lines. When filled with ink, the lines of the design will reproduce a copy on paper. **2** make drawings or designs by this method. **3** impress deeply; fix firmly: *Her face was etched in my memory. v.* [*Etch* is from Dutch *etsen,* which came from German *ätzen,* meaning "to feed, etch."] —**etch'er,** *n.*

fu ture (fyü'chər), **1** time to come; what is to come; what will be: *You cannot change the past, but you can do better in the future.* **2** that is to come; that will be; coming: *We hope your future years will be happy.* **3** chance of success or prosperity: *She has a job with a future.* **4** expressing something expected to happen or exist in time to come: *the future tense of a verb.* **5** the verb form with *shall* or *will* that expresses something taking place in time to come. "I shall go" or "I will go" is the future of "I go." 1,3,5 *n.,* 2,4 *adj.*

hol ler (hol′ər), INFORMAL. **1** cry or shout loudly. **2** a loud cry or shout. 1 *v.*, 2 *n.*

home stead (hōm′sted′), **1** house with its buildings and grounds; farm with its buildings. **2** public land granted to a settler under certain conditions by the United States government. **3** take and occupy as a homestead: *He homesteaded 160 acres of land.* 1,2 *n.*, 3 *v.*

hum ble (hum′bəl), **1** low in position or condition; not important or grand: *They lived in a humble, one-room cottage.* **2** not proud; modest: *a humble heart, to be humble in spite of success.* **3** make humble; make lower in position, condition, or pride: *humbled by defeat.* 1,2 *adj.*, **hum bler, hum blest;** 3 *v.*, **hum bled, hum bling.** [*Humble* came into English about 700 years ago from French *humble,* and can be traced back to Latin *humus,* meaning "earth."] —**hum′ble ness,** *n.* —**hum′bler,** *n.*

im mi grant (im′ə grənt), person who comes into a country or region to live there: *Canada has many immigrants from Europe. n.*

lib er ty (lib′ər tē), **1** condition of being free; freedom; independence: *The American colonies won their liberty.* **2** right or power to do as one pleases; power or opportunity to do something: *liberty of speech.* **3** permission granted to a sailor to go ashore. **4** right of being in, using, etc.: *We give our dog the liberty of the yard.* **5** too great freedom: *The author took liberties with the facts to make the story more interesting. n.,* *pl.* **lib er ties.** [*Liberty* came into English about 600 years ago from French *liberté,* and can be traced back to Latin *liber,* meaning "free."] **at liberty, 1** free: *The escaped lion is still at liberty.* **2** allowed; permitted: *You are at liberty to make any choice you please.* **3** not busy: *The doctor will see us as soon as she is at liberty.*

a	hat	i	it	oi	oil	ch	child	ə	stands for:
ā	age	ī	ice	ou	out	ng	long		a in about
ä	far	o	hot	u	cup	sh	she		e in taken
e	let	ō	open	ú	put	th	thin		i in pencil
ē	equal	ô	order	ü	rule	₮H	then		o in lemon
ėr	term					zh	measure		u in circus

noose (nüs), **1** a loop with a slip knot that tightens as the string or rope is pulled. Nooses are used especially in lassos and snares. **2** a snare or bond. **3** catch with a noose; snare. 1,2 *n.*, 3 *v.*, **noosed, noos ing.**

ob vi ous (ob′vē əs), easily seen or understood; clear to the eye or mind; not to be doubted; plain: *It is obvious that two plus two make four. adj.* —**ob′vi ous ly,** *adv.* —**ob′vi ous ness,** *n.*

prair ie (prer′ē), a large area of level or rolling land with grass but few or no trees. *n.*

prairie

proc la ma tion (prok′lə mā′shən), an official, public announcement: *a proclamation ending the war. n.*

rage (rāj), **1** violent anger: *a voice quivering with rage.* **2** be furious with anger. **3** talk or act violently; move, proceed, or continue with great violence: *Keep your temper; don't rage. A storm is raging.* **4** what everybody wants for a short time; the fashion: *Red ties were all the rage last season.* 1,4 *n.,* 2,3 *v.,* **raged, rag ing.** —**rag′ing ly,** *adv.*

rec og nize (rek′əg nīz), **1** know again: *You have grown so much that I scarcely recognized you.* **2** identify: *recognize a person from a description.* **3** acknowledge acquaintance with; greet: *recognize a person on the street.* **4** acknowledge; accept; admit: *They recognized and did their duty.* **5** take notice of: *The delegate waited till the chairman recognized her.* **6** show appreciation of.
7 acknowledge and agree to deal with: *For some years other nations did not recognize the new government.* v., **rec og nized, rec og niz ing.**

re veal (ri vēl′), **1** make known: *Never reveal my secret.* **2** display; show: *Her smile revealed her even teeth.* v. —**re veal′a ble,** *adj.* —**re veal′er,** *n.*

risk (risk), **1** chance of harm or loss; danger: *If you drive carefully, there is no risk of being fined.* **2** expose to the chance of harm or loss: *You risk your neck trying to climb that tree.* **3** take the risk of: *She risked defeat in running against the popular candidate.* 1 *n.,* 2,3 *v.*
run a risk or **take a risk,** expose oneself to the chance of harm or loss.

roam (rōm), **1** go about with no special plan or aim; wander: *roam through the fields.* **2** wander over. *v.*

ro de o (rō′dē ō *or* rō dā′ō), **1** a contest or exhibition of skill in roping cattle, riding horses and steers, etc. **2** (in the western United States) the driving of cattle together. *n., pl.* **ro de os.**
[*Rodeo* was borrowed from Spanish *rodeo,* which comes from *rodear,* meaning "go around," and can be traced back to Latin *rota,* meaning "wheel."]

sense (sens), **1** power of an organism to know what happens outside itself. Sight, hearing, touch, taste, and smell are senses. *A dog has a keen sense of smell.* **2** feeling: *The extra lock on the door gives us a sense of security.* **3** be aware; feel; understand: *I sensed that he was tired.* **4** understanding; appreciation: *He has a delightful sense of humor.* **5** Usually, **senses,** *pl.* normal, sound condition of mind: *They must be out of their senses to climb that steep cliff.* **6** judgment; intelligence: *She had the good sense to stay out of the argument. Common sense would have prevented the accident.* **7** meaning: *What sense does the word have in this sentence?* 1,2,4-7 *n.,* 3 *v.,* **sensed, sens ing.**
in a sense, in some respects; to some degree.
make sense, have a meaning; be understandable; be reasonable: *The statement "Cow cat bless Monday" doesn't make sense.*

slat (slat), a long, thin, narrow piece of wood or metal. *n.*

slough (slou *for 1;* slü *for 2*), **1** a soft, deep, muddy place. **2** a swampy place; marshy inlet; slew; slue. *n.*

spokes per son (spōks′pėr′sən), person who speaks for another or others. *n.*

rodeo

stam pede (stam pēd′), **1** a sudden scattering or headlong flight of a frightened herd of cattle, horses, etc. **2** any headlong flight of a large group: *a stampede of a panic-stricken crowd from a burning building.* **3** scatter or flee in a stampede. **4** a general rush: *a stampede to newly discovered gold fields.* **5** make a general rush. **6** cause to stampede. 1,2,4 *n.,* 3,5,6 *v.,* **stam ped ed, stam ped ing.** [*Stampede* comes from Mexican Spanish *estampida.*] —**stam ped′a ble,** *adj.* —**stam ped′er,** *n.* —**stam ped′ing ly,** *adv.*

a hat	i it	oi oil	ch child	ə stands for:
ā age	ī ice	ou out	ng long	a in about
ä far	o hot	u cup	sh she	e in taken
e let	ō open	ů put	th thin	i in pencil
ē equal	ô order	ü rule	ᴛʜ then	o in lemon
ėr term			zh measure	u in circus

wade (wād), **1** walk through water, snow, sand, mud, or anything that hinders free motion. **2** make one's way with difficulty: *Must I wade through that dull book?* **3** cross or pass through by wading: *wade a stream. v.,* **wad ed, wad ing.** **wade into,** INFORMAL. attack or go to work upon vigorously.

wid ow (wid′ō), **1** woman whose husband is dead and who has not married again. **2** make a widow of: *She was widowed when she was only thirty years old.* 1 *n.,* 2 *v.*

stampede

stin gy (stin′jē), **1** unwilling to spend or give money; not generous: *He tried to save money without being stingy.* **2** scanty; meager. *adj.,* **stin gi er, stin gi est.**

strict (strikt), **1** very careful in following a rule or in making others follow it: *The teacher was strict but fair.* **2** harsh; severe: *a strict parent, strict discipline.* **3** exact; precise; accurate: *She told the strict truth.* **4** perfect; complete; absolute: *The secret was told in strict confidence. adj.* —**strict′ly,** *adv.* —**strict′ness,** *n.*

acknowledgments

Text

Page 6: "An Errand to Town" from *The Long Winter* by Laura Ingalls Wilder, illustrated by Garth Williams. Text copyright 1940 by Laura Ingalls Wilder, renewed © 1968 by Roger L. MacBride. Pictures copyright © 1953 by Garth Williams, renewed 1981 by Garth Williams. Reprinted by permission of HarperCollins Publishers.
Page 18: *Samuel's Choice* by Richard Berleth, illustrated by James Watling. Text © 1990 by Richard J. Berleth. Illustrations © 1990 by James Watling. Used by permission of Albert Whitman & Company.
Page 42: "The Mysterious Mr. Lincoln" from *Lincoln: A Photobiography* by Russell Freedman. Copyright © 1987 by Russell Freedman. Reprinted by permission of Clarion Books, a Houghton Mifflin Company.
Page 50: "Looking for the Man Behind the Myth," by Russell Freedman. Copyright © 1991 by Russell Freedman.
Page 54: "A Cow Herder on Horseback" from *Cowboys of the Wild West* by Russell Freedman. Copyright © 1985 by Russell Freedman. Reprinted by permission of Clarion Books, a Houghton Mifflin Company.
Page 55: Lyrics from "I Am Fur From My Sweetheart," collected, adapted, and arranged by John A. Lomax and Alan Lomax. TRO - Copyright 1938 (renewed) Ludlow Music, Inc., New York, NY. Used by permission.
Page 62: From *We Pointed Them North*, by E. C. ("Teddy Blue") Abbott and Helena Huntington Smith. New edition copyright © 1955 by the University of Oklahoma Press. Reprinted by permission.
Page 64: Excerpt from *Hector Lives in the United States Now* by Joan Hewett, photos by Richard Hewett. Text copyright © 1990 by Joan Hewett. Photographs copyright © 1990 by Richard R. Hewett. Reprinted by permission of HarperCollins Publishers.
Page 70: "Anastasia" by Shannon Liffland from *Passport to Literacy: Many Stories,* New York State Reading Association, copyright © 1990. Reprinted by permission.
Page 72: "Saigon of Vietnam" by Linh To Sinh My Bui from *Stone Soup: the magazine by children.* Copyright © 1990 by the Children's Art Foundation. Reprinted by permission.
Page 74: "My moccasins have not walked" by Duke Redbird from *Red on White: The Biography of Duke Redbird* by Marty Dunn. Reprinted by permission of Stoddart Publishing Company Limited, 34 Lesmill Rd., Don Mills, Ontario, Canada.
Page 76: "Pecos Bill's Widow-Maker" is reprinted with permission of Charles Scribner's Sons, an imprint of Macmillan Publishing Company, from *If You Had a Horse* by Margaret Hodges. Copyright © 1984 by Margaret Hodges.
Page 94: "Speaking of Uncle Remus," by Julius Lester. Copyright © 1991 by Julius Lester.
Page 96: "Brer Rabbit Goes Back to Mr. Man's Garden" from *The Tales of Uncle Remus: The Adventures of Brer Rabbit* by Julius Lester, illustrated by Jerry Pinkney. Text copyright © 1987 by Julius Lester. Illustrations copyright © 1987 by Jerry Pinkney. Reprinted by permission of the publisher, Dial Books for Young Readers.

Page 104: *Her Seven Brothers* by Paul Goble. Copyright © 1988 by Paul Goble. Reprinted by permission of Bradbury Press, an affiliate of Macmillan, Inc.

Artists

Illustrations owned and copyrighted by the illustrator. Garth Williams, 6–17
James Watling, 18–41
Holly Dickens (lettering), 72
Chris Sheban, 74
Mike McGurl, 76–93
Jerry Pinkney, 96–103
Paul Goble, 104–116

Freelance Photography

Cover: Courtesy Bill Burlingham
Page 72: Chuck Shotwell
Photographs not listed were shot by ScottForesman.

Photographs

Page 42: Courtesy Chicago Historical Society
Page 45: Courtesy Library of Congress
Page 46: Courtesy Illinois State Historical Library
Page 49TL: Courtesy The Lincoln Museum, Fort Wayne, Indiana, a part of Lincoln National Corporation
Page 49TR & BL: Courtesy Library of Congress
Page 49BR: Courtesy National Portrait Gallery, Smithsonian Institution
Page 51: Courtesy Russell Freedman
Page 54: Courtesy Montana Historical Society
Page 57: Courtesy Library of Congress
Page 60: Courtesy Western History Collections/University of Oklahoma Library
Page 63: Courtesy Library of Congress
Pages 64–69: Courtesy Richard Hewett Photography
Page 94: Courtesy Julius Lester
Page 123T: Courtesy Moonmouse Collection, University of Oregon
Pages 123B, 125: Courtesy Allan Roberts
Page 126: Courtesy Bob Daemmrich/Stock Boston
Page 127: *Mustang Stampede*—Charles Russell—Woolaroc Museum, Bartelsville, Oklahoma. Photo Courtesy Joe Van Wormer

Glossary

The contents of the Glossary entries in this book have been adapted from *Intermediate Dictionary,* Copyright © 1988 Scott, Foresman and Company; and *Advanced Dictionary,* Copyright © 1988 Scott, Foresman and Company.